Kirsty Murray

Topsy-turvy wrld

HOW AUSTRALIAN ANIMALS

PUZZLED EARLY EXPLORERS

NATIONAL LIBRARY OF AUSTRALIA

Contents

ECHIDNA

17

THYLACINE

23

TASMANIAN DEVIL

29

COMMON WOMBAT

43

GREY-HEADED FLYING FOX

49

EMU

55

SUPERB LYREBIRD

73

FRILLED LIZARD

79

SEA DRAGON

83

Introduction

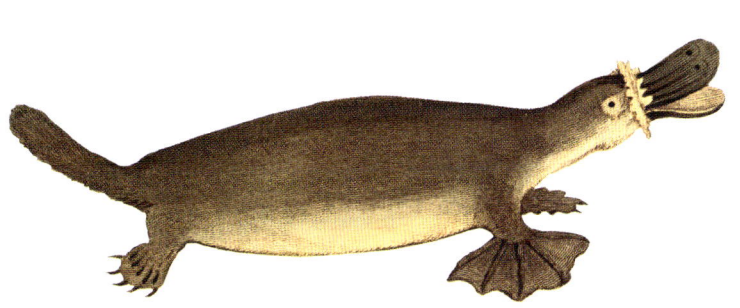

To the first Europeans who came to Australia, everything about the new land was topsy-turvy. Christmas was in summer instead of winter. Trees shed their bark instead of their leaves. The smells, sounds and tastes of the new land were nothing like Europe. Everything they assumed about the way the world was made was turned inside out and upside down.

In Australia, convicts could become policemen, beggars became rich landowners, and animals that no-one had ever imagined bounded across the landscape. Australian animals were so puzzling that European scientists questioned everything they had thought was true about the history of the natural world.

'Extraordinary', 'intriguing', 'eccentric', 'peculiar', 'curious' and 'remarkable' were the words Europeans used to describe the animals of the new world. They struggled to find names for them in English. Often, they used names of animals that they knew from the old world. Dingoes were called dogs, koalas were bears, bandicoots were rats or rabbits, and echidnas were porcupines. No-one quite knew how to describe the platypus.

'Extraordinary', 'intriguing', 'eccentric', 'peculiar', 'curious' and 'remarkable'

There was nothing really new about Australian animals. In fact, many species were among the most ancient and enduring animals the world had known. Aboriginal people had names for them in their own languages that were thousands of years old. For the Aboriginal people, it was the Europeans who were topsy-turvy with their pale skin and strange customs.

Eventually, after generations of children were born in Australia, the settlers grew to feel truly Australian. The topsy-turvy world had become their home.

Kangaroo

was known as {KANGOOROO}

10 JUNE 1770

Joseph Banks was just nodding off to sleep when a sickening crunch made him sit bolt upright in his bed. The *Endeavour* shuddered and a cry of alarm went up through the ship. Banks made his way up on deck and joined the officers to hear the terrible news.

'The most extraordinary and striking animal which the Southern Hemisphere has yet exhibited to our view ...'

George Shaw
BRITISH ZOOLOGIST, 1796

'She's stuck fast upon a reef,' said a sailor, his face pale.

A few moments later, the ship lurched and beat violently against the reef, as if to confirm the terrible news. The officers of the ship were cool in the face of disaster, but Banks knew they were hours from shore and everyone's life was at risk. By the light of the moon he could see the wreckage of the boards and keel floating on the surface of the ocean.

The *Endeavour* had struck a section of the Great Barrier Reef, off the coast of what is now Queensland, and was about to be shipwrecked. Captain James Cook and his crew spent an exhausting week manning the pumps, throwing cannons overboard to lighten the ship, and carefully steering it towards shore. On 17 June 1770, Captain Cook managed to sail up a river, now called the Endeavour River, and beach his ship for repairs.

👉 **John Hunter, Governor of New South Wales, drew this picture sometime between 1788 and 1790.**

THE MYSTERIOUS GREYHOUND

While Cook supervised the repairs of the ship, Banks set about gathering plant and animal specimens. A group of men who were sent across the river to shoot pigeons returned to the camp, describing a swift, grey creature they'd seen racing into the bush. Banks made notes in his journal about the sighting.

A couple of days later, Captain Cook stopped Banks for a conversation.

'Here, Banks,' said Cook, 'I spotted one of those animals the men spoke of the other day. It wasn't so much grey as a light mouse colour and the full size of a greyhound.'

'Do you think it was a wild dog?' asked Banks.

'It was shaped in every respect like one with a long tail which it carried like a greyhound. But for its walking, or rather running, it jumped. Jumped like a hare or a deer! Most unusual. One of the men said they had very small legs and the print of the foot was like a goat. Not that I had the chance to see their prints or their legs. The grass was too long.'

'The "dog" had a long tail, as long as any greyhound'

Banks couldn't wait to see the new creature. The next day, he set out to gather plants and kept an eye out for native animals, too. As he crouched down to examine a plant, he heard a rustling and froze. Looking up, he saw an animal a short distance away. Banks could hardly believe his eyes. The 'dog' had a long tail, as long as any greyhound, but he'd never seen anything like it before.

Back at the ship, Banks talked to the men about organising a hunting party. He was determined to catch one of the long-tailed animals. His hunting party included his own two greyhounds who were

Kangaroos are the largest hopping animals in the world. They have powerful hind legs and long, strong tails that help them keep their balance. Some European artists found it hard to understand the shape of the animal and drew it to look more like a rat or a rabbit.

fast runners. The group walked many miles over the coastal flats only to be disappointed. The jumping animals were too fast and could easily outrun Banks' greyhounds. While the greyhounds struggled through the long grass, the strange creature simply bounded over the tops and was quickly out of sight.

It would be a full week before they finally managed to shoot one of the bounding 'greyhounds'. They prepared it for dinner the next day. Banks was not impressed with the flavour, but Captain Cook thought it as good as roast beef.

By the time they managed to get the *Endeavour* repaired and out to sea again, they discovered that the Aboriginal people called the swift, bounding animal a kangooroo, or kanguru. The most famous of Australian marsupials was about to capture the imagination of the world.

Joseph Banks is the tiny figure in the background of this painting, chasing kangaroos at Endeavour River with his greyhounds. Despite having spent time at Botany Bay in New South Wales, Banks didn't see any kangaroos until he was shipwrecked in Queensland. This may be because kangaroos tend to graze during the early morning or late afternoon and evening, seeking shade in the heat of the day.

At an animal exhibition in London in 1806, a writer called M. Thomas Smith witnessed a struggle between a male kangaroo and its keeper. The big roo kicked with its hind legs and shoved with its forearms until the keeper let it return to be with a female kangaroo. Soon after, Smith published a children's book in France in which he included a picture of the scene but with boxing gloves on the male kangaroo.

LE KANGURO.

THE BOXING KANGAROO

The new marsupials caused a sensation in England. Even though a Dutch illustrator had drawn a picture of a wallaby from Indonesia 60 years earlier, it wasn't until the 1790s that illustrations of kangaroos and wallabies started to appear in books and newspapers across Europe. Children's books soon featured kangaroos with their pouches stuffed full of babies.

Live kangaroos were taken back to England and put on display in central London. The kangaroo adapted well to captivity, and some were even kept in the royal domains. By the 1820s, kangaroos could be found in public and private zoos, museums, displays and circuses from England to Russia.

Around the beginning of the twentieth century, kangaroos began to feature in circuses and sideshows around the world. Although kangaroos have weak forearms, they were kitted out with boxing gloves. By the time of the First World War, the kangaroo had become a symbol of the Australian fighting spirit.

Although some early drawings of kangaroos show them having a pouch full of babies, kangaroos only carry one joey at a time.

European artists were fascinated by the kangaroo. Some cartoonists used the kangaroo to poke fun at politicians.

AN EXTRAORDINARY ANIMAL.

When Joseph Banks returned to England, he gave a stuffed kangaroo to the painter George Stubbs. Stubbs' painting became famous and was copied by many other artists, such as this engraver, even though it wasn't very accurate.

WHAT THE EUROPEANS NEEDED TO LEARN

Joseph Banks took three specimens of the 'kangooroo' back to England. In fact, only one was actually a kangaroo, probably an eastern grey kangaroo.

The other two were wallabies. There are more than 40 species of kangaroos and wallabies, all belonging to a large family of marsupials called macropods (which means big feet). Macropods also include wallaroos, pademelons and quokkas. Kangaroos and wallabies come in many sizes and colours, including shades of red, grey, brown and yellow. The red kangaroo is the largest marsupial still alive.

The three most common kangaroos in Australia are the red kangaroo and the eastern and western grey kangaroos, but kangaroos and wallabies occur all over Australia and even in New Guinea.

The red kangaroo can travel up to 70 kilometres per hour over short distances but it can maintain a speed of about 20 kilometres per hour over long distances. No wonder Joseph Banks' greyhounds had trouble catching one!

Female kangaroos are usually pregnant, even when carrying a joey, but they have the very rare ability to stop the embryo growing in their womb until the joey in their pouch is ready to face the world. This happens especially during droughts or bad seasons.

Kangaroos are some of the few native animals that are more abundant now than before the Europeans arrived in Australia.

RED KANGAROO

KANGAROO

FAST FACTS

Common name:
red kangaroo, eastern grey kangaroo, western grey kangaroo

Scientific names:
Macropus rufus (red kangaroo), Macropus giganteus (eastern grey), Macropus fuliginosis (western grey)

Some historical names:
plains kangaroo, blue flyer; forester, scrub kangaroo; sooty kangaroo, stinker

Male:
bucks, boomers, jacks, old men

Female:
does, flyers, jills

Some Indigenous names:
kangooroo, kanguru, gangurru, arinya, arrurra, bamburr, woora, munthu

Weight and size:
depends on species and gender; 28 kg and 175 cm for a female western grey kangaroo; up to 85 kg and 240 cm for a male red kangaroo

Size relative to a 2-metre-tall man:

Habits:
generally live in mobs (except for some males) and move around to where food is plentiful

Habitat:
depends on species; some prefer grasslands, others prefer forests or even rocky ground

KANGAROO

Diet:
herbivorous — eats grasses and herbs, especially the green tips

Reproduction:
Female kangaroos carry one joey in their pouch for up to seven months.

Life span in the wild:
up to 15 or 20 years

Platypus

was known as {WATER MOLE}

LONDON, 1799

George Shaw opened the latest parcel to arrive from New Holland and his eyes grew wide. It was from the governor of New South Wales, John Hunter, but surely someone was trying to trick him. What lay in the folds of paper and cloth had to be a hoax.

'It was impossible not to entertain some distant doubts as to the genuine nature of the animal.'

George Shaw
BRITISH ZOOLOGIST, 1800

Shaw smoothed out the pages of the letter and stared at the strange sketch and the leathery skin that had been sent to him. Governor Hunter claimed to have seen an Aboriginal guide kill the animal with a spear. Shaw shook his head. He had read Hunter's journal about Port Jackson and Norfolk Island, as well as his book *The Voyage of Governor Phillip to Botany Bay*, so he knew that John Hunter had discovered many strange new animals, but this latest New World creature was simply too bizarre to believe. As a naturalist, Shaw had studied some very peculiar creatures but he had never seen anything like the *Ornithorhyncus paradoxus*. It really was a paradox. Was it a beast or a bird?

'this latest New World creature was simply too bizarre to believe'

Shaw was often sent fanciful animals that Chinese taxidermists had stitched together. Fish and monkeys were cut up and sewn into one piece, then sold to simple-minded sailors who thought they were mermaids. Shaw studied the skin of this new animal but could see no sign of stitching, even when he got out his scissors and had a good prod at all the joints. The beast had a broad flat tail and webbed feet. It looked as if the beak of a duck had been stuck onto the head of a four-legged animal. The duckbill was smoothly joined to the pelt. How on earth had they done it? Shaw stared in disbelief and turned back to John Hunter's notes. Maybe such a creature really did exist.

The first pictures of platypuses often had heads and bills that were too small, oversized feet, and bodies that were too long.

FROM ANCIENT TIMES TO THE NEXT BIG THING

Once the Europeans accepted that such a strange creature
really did exist, platypuses became all the rage back in England.
Thousands of platypuses were caught and killed.

Because platypuses hunt at night, it is rare to see them sitting on riverbanks in daylight hours. They are also very solitary animals and prefer to live alone.

Rugs were made from their thick fur, and other parts of the animal were pickled in spirits and displayed as curiosities. European naturalists were baffled. The platypus had venom in spurs on its feet, a duck's bill, a beaver's tail and feet like an otter. Was it a mammal that gave birth to live babies or did it lay eggs like a bird or a reptile? It took nearly 100 years for European scientists to solve the mystery and prove that the platypus really did lay eggs.

'The platypus had venom in spurs on its feet'

Although Europeans thought that the platypus was something new, its ancestors go back 110 million years to the time when dinosaurs roamed the earth. Fossils belonging to an ancient platypus have been found in Argentina and date back 60 million years to when Australia and South America were still joined as part of the ancient southern landmass Gondwana.

According to one Aboriginal legend, when a young duck strayed from her sheltered river pond and wandered downstream, she met a lonely water rat. The water rat threatened her with his spear and forced her to mate with him. When the duck's babies were hatched, they had their mother's duckbill but they also had brown fur instead of feathers and four webbed feet. And on each of the male's hind legs was a sharp spike, just like the spear of his father, the water rat. The duck's babies were the very first platypuses.

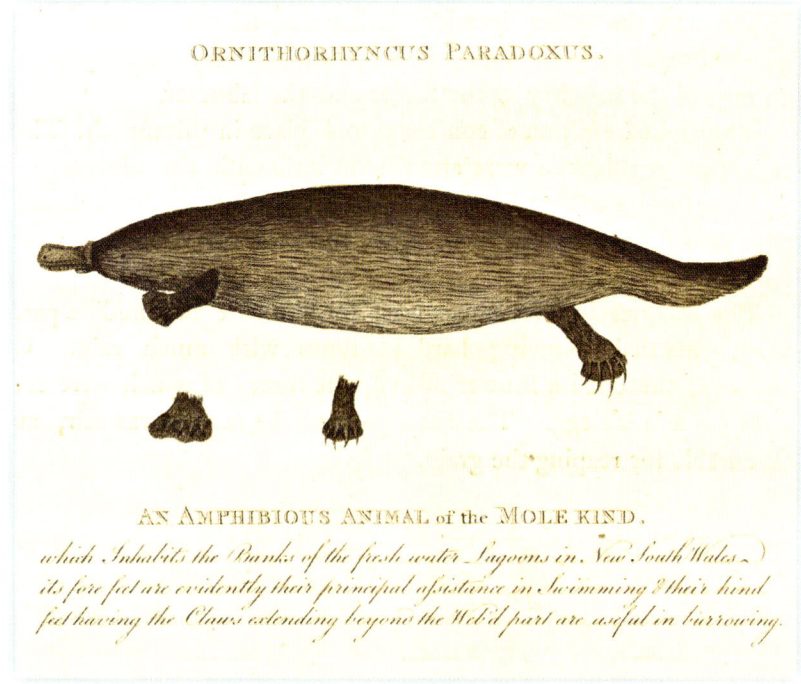

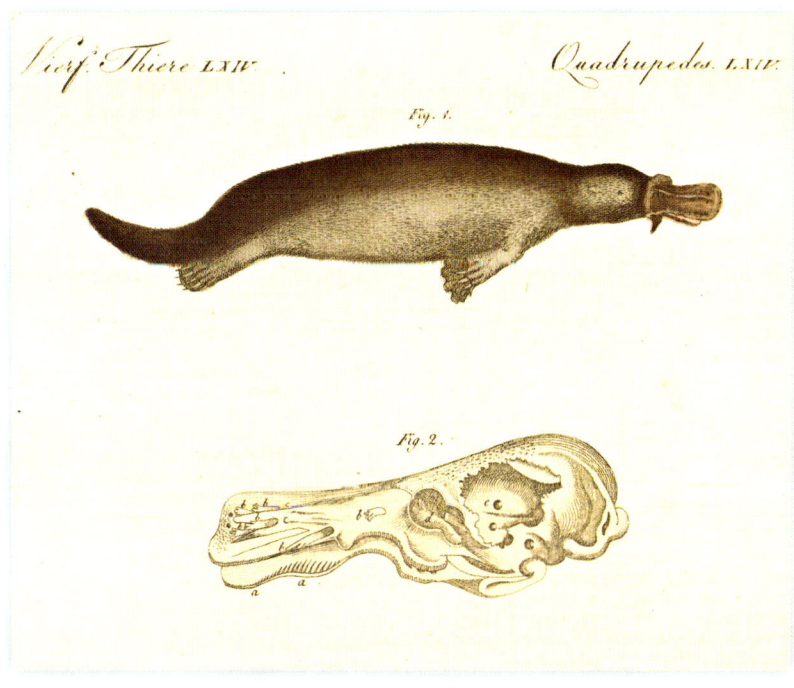

Platypuses' bodies are covered with two layers of waterproof brown fur: an inner layer of fine hair that traps air and keeps the animal warm, and an outer layer of longer flat hair.

WHAT THE EUROPEANS NEEDED TO LEARN

Platypuses dig their burrows in the banks of creeks, rivers and dams in eastern Australia, from Queensland to Tasmania.

The entrance to the burrow is just above water level and often well hidden by plant roots. Each platypus has a number of burrows within their home range to make sure they always have a safe refuge.

Platypuses hunt under water, mostly at night. They keep their eyes and ears closed but can catch fast-moving prey such as shrimps because their bills have special sensors called electro-receptors. The electro-receptors can feel tiny flickers of movement in the water around the platypus.

'THEIR BILLS HAVE SPECIAL SENSORS CALLED ELECTRO-RECEPTORS'

Using their broad tails, they dive in search of food but regularly surface to breathe. Their tail serves as a rudder to stir the water and stores fat for when food is scarce.

Every platypus has to eat about one-third of its body weight every night just to survive. They store their food in cheek pouches until they come to the surface. As adult platypuses don't have any teeth, they push the food back into their mouths and crush it between their jaws. Very young platypuses do have teeth, but they fall out soon after the young platypus first enters the water.

Adult male platypuses have a pointed spur above the heel of each hind leg. The spurs look like fangs and contain poison which can injure anyone who annoys them. Although platypus venom can kill other animals, it is not life threatening to a healthy human. A platypus sting, however, can be very painful. Platypuses make a low growling sound when angry and can be dangerous, so if you do meet one while wading in a river or creek, leave it alone.

PLATYPUS

PLATYPUS
FAST FACTS

Common name:
platypus

Scientific name:
Ornithorhynchus anatinus

Some historical names:
water mole, duckbill, duckmole

Some Indigenous names:
mallangong, tambreet, boonaburra, baarlijan, gayadar, theen-who-ween

Weight and size:
up to 2.4 kg; males up to 55 cm in total length; females up to 47 cm

Size relative to a 2-metre-tall man:

Habits:
solitary (this means the animal lives alone); mostly nocturnal (active at night); can spend up to a minute under water catching food before coming to the surface to eat it

Habitat:
lives in freshwater lakes, rivers and larger streams

PLATYPUS

Diet:
insects, worms, small fishes and frogs

Reproduction:
The female has a nest burrow with a chamber lined with water weed. She lays two eggs in late winter or spring and curls around them to incubate them for about 10 days. After they hatch, the baby platypuses suck milk from two patches on their mother's belly for up to five months. She leaves them in the burrow when she hunts.

Life span in the wild:
under 10 years

Echidna

TASMANIA, 1792

Gunshots echoed loudly across Adventure Bay and the bush grew still. For a moment, the birds fell quiet. Captain William Bligh had moored his ship off the coast of Van Diemen's Land and come ashore to hunt and investigate the heavily forested country.

> The echidna fascinated naturalists. Was it a link between the porcupine and the anteater?

He wasn't sure what, exactly, his officer had just shot. It was a small, dark and rather prickly looking animal, and he hoped at least it would be tasty. Fresh meat was always something to look forward to when coming ashore during a long voyage, even if sometimes you couldn't be sure what sort of creature you were actually eating.

George Tobin, third lieutenant on Bligh's ship the *Providence*, knelt down to examine the animal but he struggled to find the right words to describe it.

'Perhaps it's some kind of sloth,' he said. 'We could try roasting it—like a pig.'

It was difficult to skin the small animal because dozens of sharp, cream-coloured quills were lodged in its brown fur. The men set about cutting the hide away from the body and cooked the creature over the coals.

'Delicious,' announced Captain Bligh, after he'd eaten a mouthful. 'Quite a delicate flavour, don't you think, Tobin?'

'Captain Bligh flattened out the spiky hide and studied it closely'

Once the captain and his men had finished eating their small portions of meat, Captain Bligh flattened out the spiky hide and studied it closely. He noticed the animal's long, thin snout, at the end of which was a small hole.

'Amongst the most curious and interesting of quadrupeds yet discovered.'

George Shaw
BRITISH ZOOLOGIST, 1792

'It's very odd,' said Captain Bligh. 'It has a tiny tongue but I don't think its mouth would admit anything bigger than a pistol ball.'

Captain Bligh sketched a picture of the animal's flattened-out skin, carefully drawing its tiny eyes and the five claws on each of its feet. The *Providence* set sail for Tahiti, and Bligh's notes on his first sighting of an echidna were all recorded in his ship's log. It would be more than a century before naturalists understood the true nature of the spiky little animal with the 'delicate flavour'.

STRANGER AND STRANGER

The more the Europeans studied the echidna, the more it confused them. It seemed closer to a mammal than the watery platypus, with whom it appeared to have some things in common, but there also seemed to be no explanation for some of its features.

In 1802, a young male echidna was dissected in London and the puzzle of the porcupine–anteater grew more complicated. The echidna had fur, so it had to be a mammal. But there were claims that it laid eggs, so that meant it had to be related to a bird or a reptile. Also, the creature had no nipples. How on earth did it feed its babies? How did it give birth to them? Some of its organs were similar to a lizard's. Scientists spent decades arguing about how to classify this strangest of Australia's wildlife.

Echidnas mainly eat termites which they catch with their long, sticky tongues.

Australian animals had so many features that were different to European animals that artists often made mistakes when drawing them. An echidna's hind paws face backwards which gives the echidna its wonky way of walking.

In the quest to try and understand the mysterious echidna, thousands were slaughtered. It took more than 100 years before a scientist, Wilhelm Haacke, curator of the South Australian Museum, proved that the echidna laid eggs. At a meeting of the Royal Zoological Society of South Australia in 1884, Haacke showed the audience a tiny broken leathery echidna egg the size of a five-cent coin. At last the mystery was solved.

An Animal shot at Adventure Bay. It had a Beak like a Duck — a thick brown coat of Hair, through which the points of numerous Quills of an Inch long, projected & were very sharp. — It was 17 Inches long & walked about 2 In.s from the Ground. — Had very small Eyes & five Claws on each foot. — It's mouth was a small opening at the end of the Bill & had a very small tongue. — W.B.

Captain William Bligh drew this picture in his journal and made notes describing the echidna he cooked and ate at Adventure Bay in 1792.

WHAT THE EUROPEANS NEEDED TO LEARN

Some European scientists thought the echidna must be a half-formed sort of animal —less developed than a proper mammal.

The echidna actually has a big brain, so although its ancestors are ancient, there is nothing primitive or simple about it. Eventually, it was discovered that the echidna lays its eggs into a sort of pouch—really just a ridge of skin—and that the mother makes milk, like all mammals. Unlike other mammals, however, the echidna has no nipples and the baby sucks up the milk from special areas of her skin inside the 'pouch'. The echidna was different enough from all the other mammals to belong to a new group called the monotremes. The platypus is the only other monotreme, and although both are also mammals, they have some of the characteristics of birds and reptiles.

'THE ECHIDNA ACTUALLY HAS A BIG BRAIN'

European scientists often chose words from Greek mythology for the names of new animals. 'Echidna' was a fierce monster that was half-woman, half-snake. She was called the 'Mother of All Monsters'. In contrast, the Australian echidna is a gentle animal, and nothing like the mythical creature. Male echidnas, like their relative the platypus, have a spur on each back foot, but unlike the platypus the spurs are blunt and they have no venom.

If disturbed, echidnas will usually curl into a ball or lower their heads and start to dig at a furious speed, until only their spiky spines can be seen. They can also wedge themselves snugly into cracks or logs by stretching their bodies.

Echidnas use their strong forepaws to open up ant and termite nests, and then stick their sensitive snouts inside. Their tongues are covered with sticky mucus so they can quickly lick up the tiny insects and crush them in their mouths.

ECHIDNA FAST FACTS

Common name:
short-beaked echidna

Scientific name:
Tachyglossus aculeatus

Some historical names:
porcupine anteater, spiny anteater, aculeated anteater

Some Indigenous names:
innar-linger, kulai, piggi-billa

Weight and size:
up to 45 cm long; weighing up to 7 kg

Size relative to a 2-metre-tall man:

Habits:
solitary, spending most of the year alone; lives in hollow logs or burrows among roots and trees

Habitat:
lives in forests, woodlands, heath, grasslands and arid environments

ECHIDNA

Diet:
termites and ants

Reproduction:
Females lay a soft leathery egg directly into their pouch. The tiny baby emerges 10 days later and suckles from pores on two milk patches. It spends about 55 days in the pouch and a further period in a burrow.

Life span in the wild:
up to 16 years, but usually only up to 10

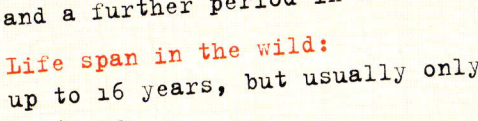
ECHIDNA

THE TASMANIAN TIGER.
(THYLACINUS CYNOCEPHALUS.)

Thylacine

was known as {ZEBRA OPOSSUM}

MID-NORTH COAST, TASMANIA, 1792

Two men stood on the deck of the *Recherche* and looked back at the dark shore of Van Diemen's Land. They had sailed from France in search of a missing French ship that had disappeared off the coast of Australia in 1788.

Although they had sailed all the way along the south coast of Australia, they still hadn't seen any sign of the lost expedition. What they did discover was a strange new world of animals and plants.

Jacques Labillardière was a French naturalist who was travelling on the *Recherche*. He had found plenty of interesting plant specimens while ashore in Van Diemen's Land, though few wild animals. However, one seaman had returned from the island with a tale of something intriguing.

'What do you think it was, this creature that you say you saw?' asked Labillardière. 'I have seen tracks on the beach myself, but I couldn't identify the animal.'

'It was like a large dog, sir,' said the seaman. 'A pale colour, streaked with black. It looked like a wild beast. Savage like.'

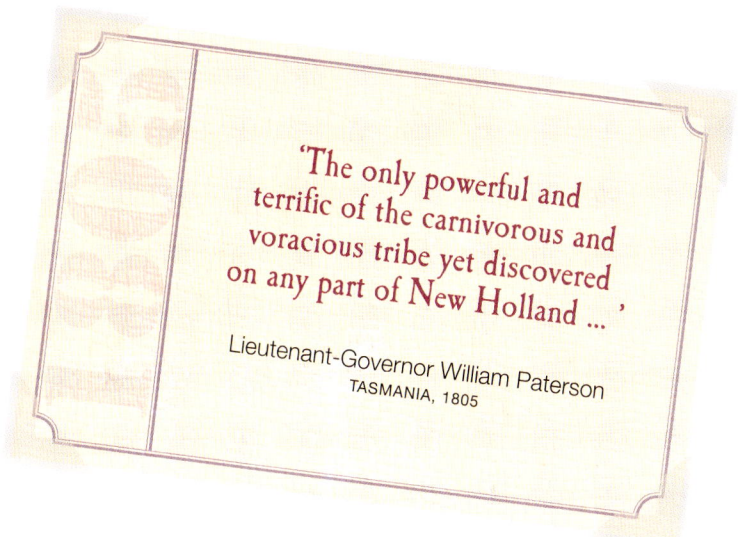

'The only powerful and terrific of the carnivorous and voracious tribe yet discovered on any part of New Holland ... '

Lieutenant-Governor William Paterson
TASMANIA, 1805

'Well, what do you think it was?' asked Labilladière. 'A wolf? A tiger? Perhaps a hyena?'

The seaman scratched his head and shrugged. 'I never saw anything like it before.'

Labillardière wrote about the mysterious creature in his journal, although he never had a chance to see the strange striped beast of Van Diemen's Land himself. The elusive 'Tasmanian tiger' was about to enter the history books. It was the beginning of the end for one of Australia's most unique and fascinating animals.

'The elusive "Tasmanian tiger" was about to enter the history books'

Some artists drew the thylacine with short legs like a possum.

FROM THE FIRST TO THE LAST

In 1805, 10 years after Labillardière reported a sighting of the striped beast, the first thylacine to be slaughtered by Europeans was killed on the mid-north coast of Tasmania. It was run to ground by a pack of dogs. Its bloody body was taken back to Hobart and shown to Lieutenant-Governor William Paterson.

Paterson could hardly contain his excitement. There had been vague sightings and rumours of a panther or wolf that prowled the forests beyond the settlement, but no-one had managed to capture or kill one. Paterson wrote to the *Sydney Gazette*: 'the form of the animal is that of a hyena, at the same time strongly reminding the observer of the appearance of a low wolf dog'.

A year later, a second 'striped wolf' was caught alive near Hobart. The naturalist George Harris

Although European settlers imagined the forests of Tasmania were full of thylacines, this was never true.

24

George Harris drew this picture. He described the animal as 'exceedingly inactive and stupid' but it was probably a young injured pup that was missing its mother.

wasn't very impressed with the animal. European settlers had begun to call the new creature a zebra opossum or a zebra wolf and had compared it to a scavenging dog. Harris examined it and wrongly named it *Didelphis cynocephali*—the dog-headed opossum. The thylacine was actually a marsupial, related to the Tasmanian devil and the quoll.

Before long, wild stories began to spread about the thylacine. One popular myth was that it was a bloodsucker that destroyed native wildlife. Another rumour claimed that it could run incredibly fast for hours. The thylacine was considered a menace to settlers and was called a savage coward. It was unfairly blamed for attacks on chickens and sheep, even though the true predators were often wild dogs introduced to Tasmania by the settlers. A bounty scheme was introduced in 1831 and 'tiger hunts' were organised to rid the countryside of the unpopular animal.

The thylacine was under threat of extinction and yet it continued to be driven out of its forest home and killed. Captured thylacines were sent to zoos around the world but would not breed in captivity. On 7 September 1936, 144 years after Jacques Labillardière stood on the deck of the *Recherche* and wondered about the illusive striped creature of Van Diemen's Land, the last-known surviving thylacine in the world died of neglect in a zoo in Hobart.

'A bounty scheme was introduced in 1831'

Occasionally, thylacines were kept in captivity, but they didn't make good pets.

Thylacinus cynocephalus, from Duncan, *Cassell's Natural History*, 1883.

This ludicrous construction involves either a miniature thylacine or a gigantic platypus.

Thylacines had a wolf-like head and grew to the size of large dogs— up to two metres in length, including their tails. Platypuses are smaller than 50 cm. The artist who drew this giant platypus (or tiny thylacine) had probably never seen any live Australian native animals.

WHAT THE EUROPEANS NEEDED TO LEARN

The thylacine was the largest marsupial predator in Australia.

It was once widespread throughout Australia and New Guinea, but died out on mainland Australia possibly as long as 2000 years ago— maybe because of competition for food from the introduced dingo.

Within decades of settlement, the thylacine was already an endangered species. Still, it was killed whenever sighted. Cash was given to anyone who presented the dead body of a Tasmanian tiger, but only eight bounties were paid out between 1849 and 1904.

Thylacines lived in small family groups and possibly had 'home ranges'. They hunted at night, often in pairs. Rather than chasing down their prey, they are now thought to have been ambush hunters, catching animals by surprise. When their pups were old enough, they would sometimes join their mother in the hunt. No-one can be sure when young thylacines became independent because the thylacine was wiped out before scientists were able to learn about its habits.

'THE THYLACINE WAS WIPED OUT BEFORE SCIENTISTS WERE ABLE TO LEARN ABOUT ITS HABITS'

We do know that the female thylacine had a backward-facing pouch in which she carried two or three young pups. The pups suckled on her milk until they were ready to leave the pouch, and then they would hunt with their parents until they were old enough to strike out on their own.

Although rumours persisted of 'Tasmanian tigers' still existing in the wild for many years after the last thylacine died, none of the sightings could be proven. Sadly, there are many things that we will never fully know or understand about the thylacine.

THYLACINE FAST FACTS

Common name:
thylacine

Scientific name:
Thylacinus cynocephalus

Some historical names:
zebra opossum, zebra wolf, Tasmanian tiger, Tasmanian wolf, zebra hyena

Some Indigenous names:
marrukurli

Weight and size:
up to 130 cm in head and body length; tail up to 65 cm long; weight up to 35 kg

Size relative to a 2-metre-tall man:

Habits:
slept in a lair by day and hunted at night, or at dawn or dusk

Habitat:
lived in the woodlands and forests of Tasmania

■ THYLACINE

Diet:
carnivorous — ate young kangaroos, wallabies and other small animals; probably also carrion (dead animals)

Reproduction:
Females carried two or three pups at a time in their pouches, leaving them in a den when they were too big for the pouch and until they were weaned.

Life span in the wild:
possibly up to seven or eight years

THYLACINE

EXTINCT

TASMANIAN DEVIL.—*Diábolus ursinus.*

Tasmanian Devil

HOBART TOWN, 1806

As evening fell, George Harris heard the devils start up again. Would the pair never stop fighting? It was the same problem every night. As darkness fell, the noise could become unbearable. Spine-chilling screeches echoed across the yard.

George Harris was assistant surveyor of the recently settled convict town of Hobart. He was also a keen naturalist and had decided to study the small, black animals that the locals called 'devils'. The devils had been easy enough to catch. They were each only the size of a small dog and their tracks were often seen on the sandy beaches of Hobart. Harris had caught two Tasmanian devils by setting traps with pieces of raw flesh. He had brought them back to his house and found an empty wooden cask to keep them in.

'their tracks were often seen on the sandy beaches of Hobart'

Harris approached the cask and lifted the lid. Inside, the male and female devils were shrieking at each other. Harris had chained them together in the hope they might soon get used to each other, but though they slept peaceably during the day, as soon as it was dark they would start to fight. His hopes of taming them as pets were fading fast. They were impossibly savage. It seemed the only good thing about the devils was that they supplied fresh meat for the convicts. He hadn't tried eating a 'devil' himself, but had heard it tasted a little like veal.

With a sense of despair, Harris stared at the devils. He then went back to his desk to continue to write up his notes about the unpleasant beasts. He was determined to write a long description of the devils and send it to the famous naturalist Joseph Banks, who lived in London. Harris had even drawn a detailed illustration of the animal and named it *Didelphis ursine*—meaning the bear opossum—though later scientists would decide the Tasmanian devil was neither a bear nor a possum.

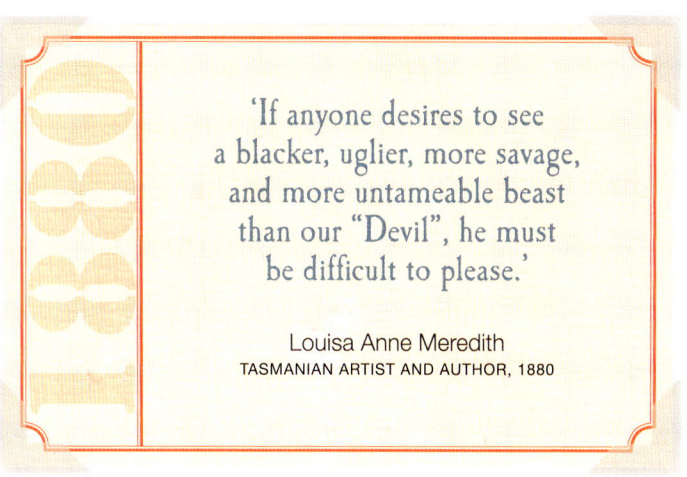

'If anyone desires to see a blacker, uglier, more savage, and more untameable beast than our "Devil", he must be difficult to please.'

Louisa Anne Meredith
TASMANIAN ARTIST AND AUTHOR, 1880

BEELZEBUB'S PUPS

Despite its small size, the European settlers quickly discovered that the Tasmanian devil could be scarily fierce.

Some of the early scientific names given to the devils, such as *Sarcophilus satanicus* (the satanic meat-lover) and *Diabolus ursinus* (the diabolical bear), showed how puzzling and frightening the Europeans found this strangely savage animal. Some settlers called them 'Beelzebub's pups' because they were considered evil creatures of the night, like the devil Beelzebub.

'they were considered evil creatures of the night'

The Tasmanian devil was common around the new settlement and created havoc by killing poultry, which didn't help its reputation. Even John Gould, a respected naturalist who usually defended Australian native animals, joined in giving the devil bad press: 'its black colouring and unsightly appearance obtained for it the trivial names of Devil and Native Devil … in its disposition it is untameable and savage in the extreme'.

The savagery of the devils soon became so legendary that by the mid–nineteenth century stories began to be told of people trapped by hordes of devils and eaten alive until nothing but a few scraps of bone were left behind. Rumours flew of large dogs being killed by packs of Tasmanian devils and reduced to nothing. Everyone imagined that the devils set upon their prey in a feeding frenzy.

The devils became famous around the world as crazy meat-eaters, and versions of the devil were drawn by cartoonists that looked nothing like real devils. The truth was, the devil was far from a fearsome hunter and was much more vulnerable than the settlers knew. Luckily, though it was hunted and poisoned, it managed to survive long enough to become a much-loved symbol of Tasmania.

Devils are a bit dog-like, with a large, broad head and very strong jaws. They have a strong smell and, as George Harris discovered, they can make amazingly loud screeches, especially when feeding.

WHAT THE EUROPEANS NEEDED TO LEARN

The Tasmanian devil belongs to a family of marsupials called Dasyurids.

It is the largest living marsupial carnivore (the thylacine would have been the largest, if it wasn't extinct).

They are a bit dog-like, with a large, broad head and very strong jaws. They have a strong smell and, as George Harris discovered, can make amazingly loud screeches, especially when feeding.

The devil is mainly a scavenger. It feeds on whatever it can find and likes to eat carrion (the bodies of dead animals). Despite its small size, the devil has a very powerful bite. Its jaws are so strong that it can snap thick bones, and its teeth are so sharp that it can eat up every part of its prey, including fur, bones and teeth. Though they mainly eat carrion, devils will hunt small mammals, birds, reptiles, frogs, insects, and even sea squirts. They grew unpopular with farmers,

'THE DEVIL IS MAINLY A SCAVENGER'

who thought they had killed sheep because they were seen feeding on sheep carcasses. In reality, because they only ate dead sheep and cattle, they actually helped keep farmland clear of flies and maggots by leaving nothing of the carcass behind.

For more than a century, devils were trapped and poisoned. No-one campaigned to save them for a very long time. In June 1941, the devils were finally protected by Tasmanian law. Slowly, they began to breed and grow in numbers. Sadly, the existence of the Tasmanian devil is now seriously under threat again, but this time from a fatal disease that curses them with horrible tumours that grow on their face. Scientists are working hard to find a cure for this terrible disease, and the race is now on to save the once unpopular devil from extinction.

TASMANIAN DEVIL

TASMANIAN DEVIL FAST FACTS

Common name:
Tasmanian devil

Scientific name:
Sarcophilus harrisii

Some historical names:
Satan's helper, Beelzebub's pup

Some Indigenous names:
tarrabah, poirinnah, par-loo-mer-rer

Weight and size:
adult males may weigh up to 12 kg and are up to 30 cm high; head and body length 65 cm; tail 26 cm; females are smaller

Size relative to a 2-metre-tall man:

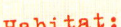

Habits:
mostly solitary, but sometimes feeds alongside other devils; active at night, sleeping in a den by day

Habitat:
occurs across much of Tasmania, from the coast to the mountains; lives in coastal heaths, open dry forests and rainforests

TASMANIAN DEVIL

Diet:
carnivorous — eats small mammals and other animals, but mainly carrion (the bodies of dead animals)

Reproduction:
The female has a den under a thick bush or in an old wombat hole. Females give birth to up to four young. The young spend about four months in their mother's backward-facing pouch, and then some more time in the den before they face the outside world.

Life span in the wild:
up to eight years

Pig-footed Bandicoot

ON THE BANKS OF THE MURRAY RIVER, JUNE 1836

One of the Aboriginal guides gave a shout. In a moment, there was a scurry of feet as a group of guides chased a small, silvery-grey animal along the banks of the river.

Thomas Mitchell watched with excitement. He'd seen the creature, too, and instantly noticed there was something unusual about it.

He called out after the guides, encouraging them to corner the little animal. It dived into a hollow tree but the men surrounded it on all sides.

'What do you call this creature?' asked Mitchell, as one of the Aboriginal guides brought him the captured animal to inspect.

'My people have no name for this. We've never seen this kind before,' said the man.

'it was the strange little front feet of the creature that drew his attention'

Mitchell took the trembling animal from the Aboriginal guide and cradled it in his hands. It was the size of a young wild rabbit and of nearly the same colour, but it had a broad head that ended in a long, slender snout, like the narrow neck of a wide bottle. And it had no tail. But it wasn't simply the lack of a tail that interested Mitchell, it was the strange little front feet of the creature that drew his attention. They were like those of a pig or a hog, with two

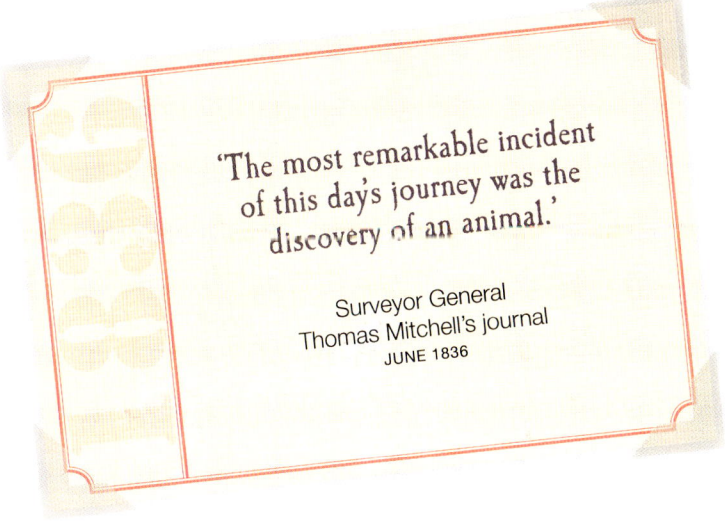

'The most remarkable incident of this day's journey was the discovery of an animal.'

Surveyor General
Thomas Mitchell's journal
JUNE 1836

small hoof-like toes. When he turned the animal over, he discovered it had a pouch like a kangaroo, but the pouch faced backwards. He couldn't wait to write about it in his journal.

Mitchell drew a picture of the little animal and sent it to a naturalist in England named William Ogilby. Like Mitchell, Ogilby was fascinated by the new bandicoot. There was no other species of bandicoot in the world that lacked a tail. Ogilby gave it the scientific name of *Chaeropus ecaudatus*, which means swine-footed and tailless.

MISERABLE AS AN ORPHAN BANDICOOT ON A BURNT RIDGE

There are nine species of bandicoot. Except for the pig-footed bandicoot, the other Australian bandicoots were not considered much of a prize by European naturalists.

They were often described as being like large brown rats. Mrs Lance Rawson's *Australian Cook and Laundry Book* (1897) warned that 'a bandicoot is a very disagreeable animal to clean, therefore it should be done as soon after killing as possible … when ready, arrange the bandicoot neatly on a dish, strain the sauce over, then serve'.

'The name "bandicoot" became linked to all sorts of unhappiness'

Because bandicoots often lived on poor tracts of land, the Europeans talked about 'land so poor that a bandicoot would starve on it', and a 'bandicoot run' was a useless bit of land. The name 'bandicoot' became linked to all sorts of unhappiness— someone might be 'miserable as an orphan bandicoot on a burnt ridge' or 'as poor/hungry/bald/blind/barmy as a bandicoot'.

The sayings about bandicoots have died out and, sadly, so have several species of bandicoot, including the beautiful little pig-footed bandicoot.

Thomas Mitchell drew this picture of the pig-footed bandicoot. He thought that the animal was born without a tail. In fact, it had lost its tail in an accident.

A TWIST IN THE TALE

In the mid-1840s, another pig-footed bandicoot was found on the Darling River, but this time the creature had a tail. Scientists decided it must be a new, tailed species, but some people doubted that a true tailless bandicoot existed.

When a zoologist from the Australian Museum showed a sketch of the tailless pig-footed bandicoot to some Aboriginal people of the Murray–Darling region and asked them to help him find a creature like it, he got more than he'd bargained for. The Aboriginal people arrived in his camp with a batch of common bandicoots with their tails twisted off. The zoologist managed to collect some pig-footed bandicoots himself, but every one of them had tails.

Eventually, the Europeans realised that the pig-footed bandicoot actually has the longest tail of all the bandicoots.

WHAT THE EUROPEANS NEEDED TO LEARN

The pig-footed bandicoot is now extinct. The species died out before we had the chance to learn much about it.

We know that it was nocturnal (active at night) and that it gave birth to two pouch young in winter. Its feet were more like the feet of a tiny deer than a pig. It probably ran on all fours rather than bounding along on two legs like other types of bandicoots.

'SEVERAL OTHER SPECIES OF BANDICOOT ARE NOW ALSO EXTINCT OR IN TROUBLE'

The arrival of cattle is possibly the main reason for the extinction of the pig-footed bandicoot. Cattle destroyed the bandicoots' nests and hiding places. As rabbits, foxes and cats began to spread into the bush, they also helped to wipe out the pig-footed bandicoot. The last specimen of a pig-footed bandicoot was collected in 1907, and the last reported sighting was in the 1950s. The stuffed pig-footed bandicoot pictured below is over 100 years old. No-one managed to take a photograph of a living pig-footed bandicoot before they became extinct.

PIG-FOOTED BANDICOOT

EXTINCT

PIG-FOOTED BANDICOOT FAST FACTS

Common name:
pig-footed bandicoot

Scientific name:
Chaeropus ecaudatus

Some historical names:
chestnut-eared chaeropus

Some Indigenous names:
none known

Weight and size:
up to 26 cm in head and body length; tail up to another 15 cm; weight unknown

Size relative to a 2-metre-tall man:

Habits:
nocturnal (active at night); by day, lived in a shallow squat in a covered nest made of twigs and grasses and lined with softer grasses; when startled from the squat, it took shelter in hollow logs or under shrubs

Habitat:
lived in open scrubby woodlands of the inland plains

PIG-FOOTED BANDICOOT

Diet:
grasses, seeds, succulent leaves and roots, insects

Reproduction:
Females carried two babies at a time in a backward-facing pouch. They made a nest of grasses in a shallow burrow.

Life span in the wild:
unknown

Koala

was known as {SLOTH}

BLUE MOUNTAINS, 1802

Francis Barrallier wasn't sure what it was that Gogy, his Aboriginal guide, was butchering. The governor of New South Wales had sent Francis, a young engineer, to explore the thick bush beyond the new settlement of Sydney.

Francis had to rely on Gogy and his companions to show him a path over the mountains. Sometimes, he had to rely on Gogy to catch his dinner, too. The animal Gogy was cutting up to cook on the camp fire looked something like a monkey or a small bear. Francis had never seen anything quite like it.

Gogy called it a 'colo' in his language. It occurred to Francis that the strange monkey would make a great trophy to give to the governor. He asked Gogy for the head of the beast, but it was too late. Either someone had already eaten it or thrown it into the bush. Francis offered two fine spears and a tomahawk in exchange for a piece of the 'colo', but all that was left were two clawed feet. Francis put the paws into a glass bottle, pickled them in spirits, and sent them back to Sydney as a gift for Governor Philip Gidley King.

'the strange monkey would make a great trophy to give to the governor'

'The sloths are the lowest form of existence in the order of animals ... one more defect and they could not have existed.'

Baron Georges de Buffon
FRENCH NATURALIST, 1772

Although the first settlers often referred to the koala as a monkey or a bear, it isn't actually related to bears or monkeys at all.

The name 'koala' comes from an Aboriginal word meaning 'no drink'. Koalas receive 90 per cent of all the fluid they need from gum leaves. The koala only drinks water when it is sick or sometimes during droughts, when there is not enough moisture in the eucalypt leaves.

In 1803, a koala was caught with two young joeys. It was the first time the early settlers had a chance to examine the new Australian 'bear' up close. Governor King finally had living examples of the animal whose paws had been sent to him by Francis Barrallier. King was keen to send the koalas back to England, but one of the captured baby koalas died within days, and the mother and other joey followed soon after. Some thought the koala lived on nuts and berries, but eventually the settlers realised that it lived on leaves alone. It wasn't until 1880 that a koala survived the long sea voyage to England.

The reaction to the koala was not enthusiastic. The early settlers had few kind words to say about the koala. It was described as 'a senseless torpid creature'. Some people called it a monkey, bear, or sloth, and wondered what had happened to its tail. An assistant surveyor working for the government described it as 'harmless-looking and pitiful … like many other animals of the colony, they are drowsy and stupid by day, but become more animated by night, and when disturbed they make a melancholy cry, exciting pity'.

Perhaps the cry of the koalas sounded unhappy because they were afraid. Koalas use a range of soft murmuring, humming, clicking or squeaking noises to communicate with each other, and they grunt or growl when they're annoyed. But when they cry out, it's usually in fear.

'they grunt or growl when they're annoyed'

Up until the early twentieth century, millions of koala furs were sold to Europe and the USA. Hundreds of thousands of koalas were shot and poisoned every year, and the forests that they lived in were cut down. Eventually, the Australian Government made it illegal to kill koalas, and the Australian people grew to love and value them. The koala became an important character in all sorts of stories for children, from Bunyip Bluegum in *The Magic Pudding* to the famous Blinky Bill.

Once they were protected, the koala population began to rise, so that there are now healthy numbers in many places in Australia. In some areas, however, koalas suffer threat from feral animals, pets, cars, disease and the destruction of their bushland homes. Life can still be tough for koalas in the wild.

The artist who drew this picture obviously didn't understand that koalas only live in eucalypt forests and are fussy about which trees they pick as favourites. Not every gum tree has leaves that suit the tastes of koalas.

WHAT THE EUROPEANS NEEDED TO LEARN

The koala is a marsupial, that special group of animals that raise their young in a pouch —common in Australia but rare in the rest of the world.

Koalas are very territorial and like to have a 'home range'. Once they've chosen their favourite tree, they stay there, munching on the leaves and sleeping in the forks of the branches.

Because leaves are very low in protein and are hard work to chew and digest, koalas need to save their energy. They move slowly and are rarely in a hurry to do anything, which is probably why the European settlers thought they were like sloths.

The koala's fur is thick and woolly, coloured either grey or grey-brown. They have strong legs and sharp claws that help them climb trees. Each of their paws includes five fingers, not unlike human hands. Koalas have fingerprints like humans and monkeys. Fingerprints are not common among mammals.

Adult females give birth to only one baby each year. Twins are very rare. The tiny baby looks like a pink jelly bean. It has no hair, no ears and is blind. Once it is old enough to peep out of the pouch, the baby starts to eat a special 'pap' made by its mother that helps it to digest eucalypt leaves. When it leaves the pouch, the young koala stays close to its mother for the next few months, often riding on her back.

KOALA

KOALA
FAST FACTS

Common name:
koala

Scientific name:
Phascolarctos cinereus

Some historical names:
New Holland sloth, koalo, koala bear

Some Indigenous names:
cola, koolah, cullawine, koolewong, colo, banjora, yarri, nargoon, nurrumpi, koob-bor, kulla

Weight and size:
64–82 cm in length; adult male up to 14 kg in southern Australia; 9 kg in northern Australia

Size relative to a 2-metre-tall man:

Habits:
arboreal (lives in trees); territorial and mostly lives alone (except for female koalas who have babies); nocturnal, eating mainly at night and sleeping or resting for up to 18 hours a day

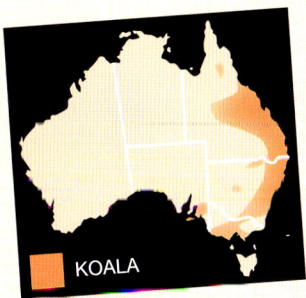

Habitat:
forests and denser woodlands of mainland eastern Australia

KOALA

Diet:
herbivorous — eats eucalypt leaves (gum leaves)

Reproduction:
Adult females usually produce one offspring per year. Babies spend six to seven months in their mother's pouch and then stay close for up to a year.

Life span in the wild:
up to 10 years for a male in the wild, but often only two to three years in more difficult habitats

Common Wombat

FURNEAUX ISLANDS, 1798

Matthew Flinders raised a hand to shield his gaze from the sun. The last survivors of the shipwreck that he had been sent to rescue were gathered on the beach, waiting for the longboats to come ashore and take them back to civilisation.

'The Wombat is a joy, a triumph, a delight, a madness.'

Dante Gabriel Rossetti
BRITISH ARTIST, PHILOSOPHER AND POET, 1869

The shipwrecked sailors had been on the island for nearly a year. Their ship, *Sydney Cove*, had been battered by a storm in the roaring forties and run aground on Preservation Island in February 1797. Preservation Island is in the Furneaux Group of islands in the eastern end of Bass Strait.

'We'll be glad to get back to Port Jackson, we will,' said one of the grateful shipwrecked sailors. 'I don't think I could stomach another of them fat badgers.'

'Badgers?' asked Flinders. He was always curious about the animals of the Great South Land.

'There's plenty of them on that neighbouring island. We take one of the longboats over and catch us a few. They're slow and they have no sense. They don't even put up a fight. Easy to catch. They taste a bit like tough mutton and there's plenty of meat on them—enough for three or four of us to eat in a day but I've had my fill of them.'

Flinders rowed over to the neighbouring island with some of his men and caught one of the 'badgers'. Just as the sailors had said, the animal was easy to catch. Flinders heaved it onto his shoulder and carried it from the island. When he sailed back to Port Jackson, he took the live wombat with him as a gift for Governor John Hunter.

In March 1798, Flinders presented the 'live badger' to the governor. The wombat refused to eat anything that was offered to it. Six weeks later it died.

John Hunter had its body preserved in spirits and shipped it to London, along with an illustration, a letter, and the skin and skull of another wombat. Hunter explained in his letter that the Aboriginal people called the animal a 'wombach', but in London they named it *Didelphis ursine* (ursine opossum) because it looked like a cross between a bear and a possum.

Wombats have strong shoulders, powerful stubby legs and sharp claws that are great for digging.

FROM THE DINNER TABLE TO FAMILY PET

The wombat had managed to escape being noticed for the first 10 years of European settlement. Once it was discovered, it quickly made its way onto the menus of sailors and sealers.

In 1802, François Péron, a French naturalist, was stranded on King Island during a squall. A sealer offered Péron and his companions shelter from the storm. He took Péron into a huge shed, where half-a-dozen emus, several kangaroos and two large wombats were hanging from meat hooks. The sealers of the islands ate almost nothing but meat, especially wombats. When the storm had settled, Péron took three live wombats back to Europe with him.

Wombats were hunted so often by whalers and sealers that they soon disappeared from all the islands of Bass Strait, except Flinders Island. The wombats of the islands were easier to catch than those on the mainland because they often foraged on the beach during the day.

> **At first, some naturalists thought that wombats climbed trees and stood on their back legs like a kangaroo. Other scientists thought that they could walk under water.**

This picture was drawn by one of the Frenchmen who visited the Bass Strait islands where sealers ate wombats. In fact, wombats only have one baby at a time and the mother raises it without any help from the father.

Eventually, unlike some other native animals, several wombats survived the trip to Europe and were made family pets in homes in England. By the mid-1850s, the wombat was a real presence in England. Despite this, there was still much confusion about the true nature of the wombat.

The famous painter and poet Dante Gabriel Rossetti collected exotic animals and kept a pair of pet wombats in his house. The wombats even attended his parties. Perhaps all the socialising was too much for the wombats, for they didn't live long.

'The wombats even attended his parties'

In 1856, a baby wombat was born in London's Zoological Gardens— the first to be born outside Australia.

WHAT THE EUROPEANS NEEDED TO LEARN

There are actually three different wombat species in Australia and they are found nowhere else.

It was the common wombat that Matthew Flinders came across in the Furneaux Islands and that Rossetti kept as a pet. Wombats like to forage for their food at night and travel across a wide area. They also love to burrow. This means they're not happy being kept as pets.

Wombat burrows can be up to 60 metres long, with several entrances and chambers. Although wombats love to dig, they usually take over very old, existing burrows. Wombats will share their burrows with other wombats but they don't like to socialise. They will snort or grunt if another wombat comes too close.

Some Europeans imagined that wombats ate everything they came across, just like a pig. They assumed that wombats even ate small animals. Wombats are, in fact, vegetarian, or more accurately herbivores, which means they eat grass, leaves, the roots of plants and occasionally bark.

Newborn wombats are tiny. They weigh only one gram and are less than three centimetres long. The baby has to crawl from its mother's birth canal into her pouch. Like many other Australian marsupials, a wombat's pouch faces backwards (only kangaroos and wallabies have forward-facing pouches). This stops dirt and twigs from getting caught in the pouch when the mother digs. After the baby wombat leaves the pouch, it may stay with its mother for up to 18 months, but their relationship may continue for years.

'NEWBORN WOMBATS ARE TINY'

COMMON WOMBAT

COMMON WOMBAT FAST FACTS

Common name:
common wombat or bare-nosed wombat

Scientific name:
Vombatus ursinus

Some historical names:
badger, ursine opossum, wombach

Some Indigenous names:
wombat (Eora language), warreen

Weight and size:
up to 1.1 m in length; weighs around 35 kg

Size relative to a 2-metre-tall man:

Habits:
mostly lives alone; feeds at night, early morning or late afternoon

Habitat:
mainly the forests of south-eastern Australia and Tasmania, often in mountainous areas

COMMON WOMBAT

Diet:
herbivorous — grazes on grasses, roots and the leaves of shrubs, occasionally bark

Reproduction:
Females give birth to one tiny baby at a time. The baby stays in its mother's pouch from between six to 14 months. After about six months it comes and goes until it leaves for good.

Life span:
up to 28 years in captivity; about 14 years in the wild, but many wombats die before six years due to mange or lack of food

Grey-headed Flying Fox

ENDEAVOUR RIVER, QUEENSLAND, 1770

'I tell you I seen it!' exclaimed the sailor. Captain Cook wasn't sure whether to believe the sailor or not. He had heard a lot of strange stories from seamen in his years as a ship's captain.

'It was as big as a one gallon cagg (keg), as black as the Devil himself and it had two horns on its head. It went but slowly but still, I dared not touch it.'

The shipwrecked *Endeavour* was still being repaired on the banks of the Endeavour River. The sailor had been out in the mangroves when he'd seen the strange creature. It was just as well he didn't see it in flight, for he would have been terrified by its great flapping black wings.

'He soon realised "the devil" was actually a large bat'

Joseph Banks also heard the sailor's description of the devil in the mangroves and went out to see it for himself. He soon realised 'the devil' was actually a large bat. Banks wrote about it in his journal, and his writings became the first record of an Australian flying fox.

'The name of Vampire Bat has been given to this fruit-eating animal, and many dismal tales of its blood-sucking propensities have been rife among the ignorant, but there is of course not a grain of truth to these statements.'

Gerard Krefft
CURATOR, AUSTRALIAN MUSEUM, 1871

Vampire bats do exist but there are none in Australia.

TWENTY THOUSAND FILTHY CREATURES

In early 1791, the settlers of Port Jackson witnessed thousands of bats swooping across the settlement. John Hunter went out to watch as more than 20 000 of them were seen within the space of a couple of kilometres.

Bats are the only mammals that can truly fly.

It was a roasting hot, dry summer. Driven by the wind, the bats covered all the trees. Normally in the evening the bats would fly southward, but the heat was so intense in the summer of 1791 that the bats dropped dead, unable to bear the burning winds. They fell to the ground and into the creek on Rose Hill. The water was tainted for days.

‘Some thought they were horrific, while others called them “filthy creatures”’

Many of the settlers were as appalled by the bats as Captain Cook's sailor. Some thought they were horrific, while others called them 'filthy creatures', and many people were afraid of them.

Not everyone was nervous of them. The governor kept one as a pet in his house, where it would hang all day by one leg. Flying foxes hang upside down because their legs are not strong enough to support them standing. One of the servants would feed the bat boiled rice, which set the bat 'lapping out of his hand like a cat'. The governor described the bat as having a face like a little fox, with wings that stretched out to over a metre from the tip of each wing.

Few settlers wanted to keep bats as pets, and explorers who were trying to map the countryside were much more interested in cooking the bats than taming them. Once they discovered that the plump fruit bat was good eating, shooting flying foxes as they hung sleepily from their perches became a common sport. Roasted flying fox became a regular part of some explorers' diets.

Grey-headed flying foxes are very large bats and their wingspan may reach to over a metre, so it's no wonder the Europeans were startled by having thousands of them fly over the new settlement.

THE VAMPIRE.

It took a long time for the term 'vampire bat' to go out of use for the flying fox.

WHAT THE EUROPEANS NEEDED TO LEARN

There are several species of flying foxes in Australia, though it was usually the grey-headed flying fox that was labelled a vampire.

It is this species that the early settlers of Port Jackson would most likely have seen, although it actually looks nothing like a vampire. The 'devil' bat that the sailor of the *Endeavour* saw was probably a black flying fox, which is common in northern and north-eastern Australia. It is almost completely black in colour, with a slight rusty red–coloured collar and a light frosting of silvery grey on its belly.

True vampire bats are tiny and feed on the blood of large animals, such as cattle. They are found only in Central and South America.

'THEY ARE STRICTLY VEGETARIAN'

Flying foxes spend their days resting in large groups or 'camps' in their favourite trees. When night falls, they fly up to 50 kilometres in search of their favourite foods, which include nectar, pollen, and fruit—not blood! They are strictly vegetarian.

Unlike many other bats, grey-headed flying foxes have a strong sense of both sight and smell. They do not navigate by sonar.

Baby flying foxes are born while their mother hangs upside down, and they cling to their mother's fur and her teat while she forages for food. When they are a bit older, she leaves them hanging in the camp while she looks for food, and then nurses them on her return. Although grey-headed flying foxes are still present in large numbers in some areas, particularly around cities, their numbers are seriously declining in other parts of Australia and they are classed as vulnerable. This means they might become extinct if we don't protect them.

GREY-HEADED FLYING FOX

GREY-HEADED FLYING FOX FAST FACTS

Common name:
grey-headed flying fox

Scientific name:
Pteropus poliocephalus

Some historical names:
vampire bat

Some Indigenous names:
wuka

Weight and size:
up to 29 cm in length; weighs around 1 kg; females slightly smaller

Size relative to a 2-metre-tall man:

Habits:
very social animals — living and foraging in colonies, especially in the warmer months when food is most plentiful; nocturnal, travelling at night in search of food; hangs upside down in favoured trees across a defined range

Habitat:
lives in forests and woodlands of eastern Australia, from central Queensland to Victoria, and in coastal and mountainous areas, including the major cities

GREY-HEADED FLYING FOX

Diet:
vegetarian — eats fruit, nectar, pollen and fruit blossoms

Reproduction:
Females give birth to one young in October or November.

Life span in the wild:
unknown

Emu

was known as {NEW HOLLAND CASSOWARY}

SYDNEY, 1802

A shot echoed across Sydney Cove. The convict lowered his gun and smiled. As the governor's game-killer, he had the best job.

He was given as much gunpowder and shot as he needed to kill the animals the governor wanted. Captain Phillip would be pleased. The convict had been given the task of shooting an emu and he'd managed to do it with a single ball.

The settlers, soldiers and convicts of the First Fleet had been in Sydney Cove for six weeks and there'd been much talk of the big, leggy birds that everyone had seen in the distance. They were so shy and ran so swiftly that no-one had managed to shoot one. When the game-killer announced his success, there were shouts of excitement as officers and men ran to where the big bird lay sprawled on the grass. It looked even bigger up close than it had at a distance.

'there'd been much talk of the big, leggy birds'

The emu was dragged back to camp, and the officers squatted down to examine it properly. Captain Arthur Phillip, the governor of the colony, was away exploring and would be sorry he missed the excitement. The bird measured seven feet two inches (218 centimetres) in height and weighed 70 pounds (32 kilograms). Its legs were long and covered with thick strong scales, but the wings hardly deserved to be called wings at all.

'Those wings, they're ridiculous. Look how small they are. And the feathers, they're so tiny.'

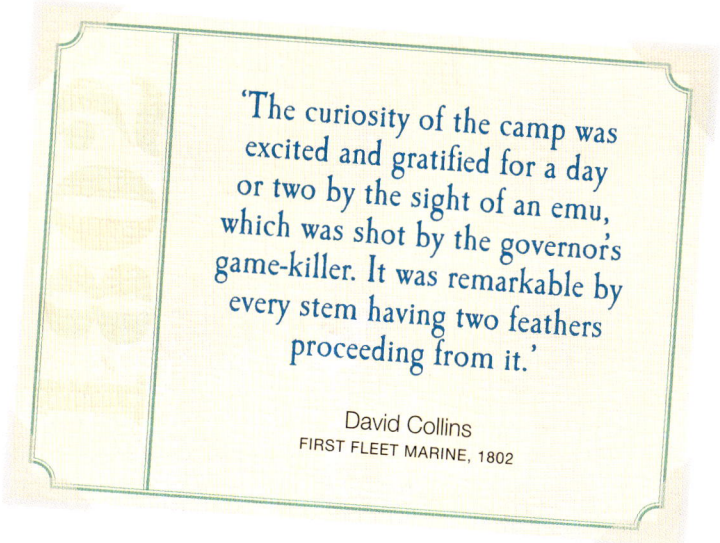

> 'The curiosity of the camp was excited and gratified for a day or two by the sight of an emu, which was shot by the governor's game-killer. It was remarkable by every stem having two feathers proceeding from it.'
>
> David Collins
> FIRST FLEET MARINE, 1802

The officers cooked up the meaty bird, and were pleased to discover that it was delicious.

'Very well flavoured,' announced David Collins, one of the marines.

'Tender as the best beef,' announced another officer.

When Captain Arthur Phillip returned, he was disappointed to have missed out on the feast. He ordered the skin of the enormous bird to be preserved in spirits. Then he sent the specimen of the new bird 'of the ostrich kind' to England, where it was stuffed and mounted and presented to the famous naturalist Joseph Banks.

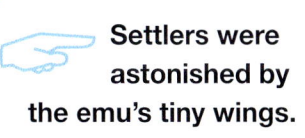
Settlers were astonished by the emu's tiny wings.

By the time John Gould painted this picture, naturalists had learned that the father emu looks after the chicks, not the mother.

FROM TRACKS TO THE COAT OF ARMS

The very first European to sight emu footprints was the Dutch explorer Willem de Vlamingh.

He wrote in his journal of seeing 'steps like those of a dog and a cassowary' and puzzled over what sort of creature could have made such huge tracks. The first Europeans to see the actual bird were the convicts and soldiers of the First Fleet.

Naturalists named it the southern cassowary and imagined that it might even grow as high as 11 feet (three metres). Rumours flew back and forth between the new settlers in Australia and scientists in England about the new super bird of the Southern Hemisphere.

The first emu egg to be found by a European was collected in March 1791. It was huge, dark green in colour, with little black specks scattered across the shell. Naturalists suggested that the giant bird could only lay one egg at a time, but later in the same year, a nest of 14 eggs was discovered.

Harvesting nests quickly became popular. The shells were used as drinking cups and the eggs made great pancakes.

'the eggs made great pancakes'

The early European settlers began to find many uses for the long-legged bird. Specially bred hunting dogs were used to catch the emu, and the number of them around Sydney Cove quickly fell. Emu fat was used for fuelling lamps, and its meat was valued as an important food source. Feathers were used for decoration, and the hides of the emus were tanned like leather.

Once crops began to be planted by the Europeans, the emu soon came to be seen as a pest. Emus were culled in their thousands. The Tasmanian emu soon disappeared from around settled areas. Luckily, there were still many emus inland as well as in coastal areas.

In 1908, the emu, along with the kangaroo, was placed on Australia's first coat of arms. Despite the pride that Australians felt in the long, leggy bird, it wasn't until the 1970s that emus in the wild became protected by law.

Emus can't fly but they can run as fast as 50 kilometres an hour for short distances.

The first European artists to draw the emu weren't sure what to do about its tiny wings and backward bending knees.

WHAT THE EUROPEANS NEEDED TO LEARN

In September 1791, one of the marines of the First Fleet wrote of chasing some 'beautifully striped' young emus and separating the chicks from their mother.

The Europeans still had a long way to go before they understood emus—the adult emu that was caring for the chicks was not their mother, but their father. The chicks were taken captive and, despite the greatest care, they soon died. They needed their father to look after them.

When Europeans finally realised that it was always the male that looked after the babies, and not the female, they were intrigued. The famous scientist Charles Darwin wrote about the emus as being the reverse of every normal bird: 'the females being savage, quarrelsome, and noisy, the males gentle, and good'.

Despite the fact that some of the early naturalists thought emus might grow to be three metres tall,

the average emu is about two metres in height, which makes them the second-tallest bird in the world, after the ostrich. Female emus are slightly larger than the male, which probably added to the confusion for the early settlers when trying to decide which emu was a male and which was a female. It was a topsy-turvy world indeed.

Although wild emus are protected, emu farms can be found in many countries of the world.

EMU AND CHICKS

EMU
FAST FACTS

Common name:
emu

Scientific name:
Dromaius novaehollandiae

Some historical names:
New Holland cassowary, cassowary of New South Wales

Some Indigenous names:
barrimal (Dja Dja Wurrung language), myoure (Gunai language) murawung or birabayin (Eora and Darug langauges), boolongena, dinewan, punnamoonta

Weight and size:
up to 2 m in height; weighs 45 kg; male slightly smaller

Size relative to a 2-metre-tall man:

Habits:
nomadic (moving from place to place); usually seen in pairs, though they can also be found in large groups

Habitat:
forests, grasslands and woodlands; used to occupy much of the mainland and Tasmania, but is now more or less absent from closely settled areas

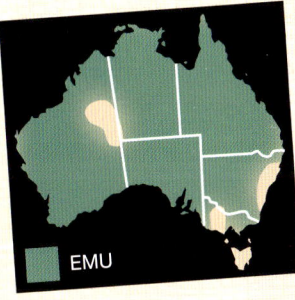

EMU

Diet:
leaves, fruit, seeds and roots of plants, and insects

Reproduction:
Emus scrape together a large, scanty nest of leaves, bark, grass and/or sticks on the ground. The female lays five to 20 (average nine) large green eggs, and the male incubates the eggs and looks after the chicks.

Life span in the wild:
up to 20 years

Black Swan

was known as *{RARA AVIS}*

WESTERN AUSTRALIA, 1697

On a hot January afternoon, Captain Willem de Vlamingh and his crew lowered their longboats into the mouth of a wide and beautiful river.

Their fleet of ships had arrived on the south-west shores of the Great South Land in late December. They had been sent by the governor of the Dutch East Indies to search for a lost ship. Instead, they found something that no-one had imagined could truly exist.

The longboats crossed the bar at the entrance of the river and began to row upstream. As the oars cut smoothly into the surface of the still blue water, the sailors looked about them in wonder. Two large black birds with beaks as red as blood were bobbing on the surface of the river.

'Are they swans?' asked one sailor.

'They can't be swans. Swans are white. Those birds, they're quite black.'

'Row faster, we can overtake them!'

The sailors hooked the pair of black swans and took them back to the ship where all the crew marvelled at the mysterious black birds. Every sailor had seen the common white swan of Europe, but to see a black swan was as strange as waking up in the morning to a green sky.

On their next trip up the river, the Dutch sailors spotted even more of the huge birds. As the swans took flight, the white-tipped end of each wing was revealed, but in every other aspect the birds were black as night.

Captain de Vlamingh named the waterway Swarte Swaane Drift (Black Swan River), in honour of the new species of swan. When he sailed back to Batavia (now Jakarta), he carried three live swans as a gift for the governor of the Dutch East Indies. The swans reached Batavia but died one by one shortly after arrival. The news of the swans was sent back to Europe and was recorded in reports in both England and Holland. The impossible was possible. Black swans really did exist.

'the crew marvelled at the mysterious black birds'

'To vulgar ears a black swan has the sound of a miracle.'

George Shaw
BRITISH ZOOLOGIST, 1789

In European mythology black animals were the companions of witches.

PURE WHITE SWAN VERSUS EVIL BLACK SWAN

For Europeans, the black swan was a mythical creature that could only have existed in ancient times, but for the Aboriginal people of Australia the black swan had been a feature of their lives and stories since the Dreamtime.

There are many different versions of the origins of the black swan across Aboriginal Australia. In one Dreamtime story from the Noongar people of Western Australia, the first two black swans were brothers who had been changed into white swans by magic. When they were attacked by eaglehawks, the blood from their wounds stained their beaks red. Just when the swans thought they were defeated, black crows, who were sworn enemies of the eaglehawks, came to their rescue. Though the eaglehawks had torn out most of the white feathers, the black crows gave their own feathers to the injured swan brothers, transforming them from white to black.

Captain de Vlamingh wasn't the first European to sight a black swan. Sixty years earlier, another Dutch skipper had mentioned one in his ship's logbook. But it wasn't until members of the First Fleet began to see black swans that Europeans realised the bird they had named '*rara avis*' (rare bird) was common in Australia.

In European fairy stories and legends, black animals were usually symbols of evil. Some early settlers couldn't accept that the Australian birds could be true swans, for swans were meant to be symbols of purity. They didn't believe that such a black creature could be related to the noble white swan.

'black animals were usually symbols of evil'

When two swans were presented to the King of England, one died and the other escaped and was shot by a game-keeper as it flew across the River Thames.

In Australia, vast numbers of black swans were killed for their soft down or for their meat, and their eggs were gathered for cooking. Some were shot simply for the pleasure of hunting them down. As swamps and marshes were drained to make way for settlements, the men who hunted the black swan and other waterfowl for a living began to worry that they would soon be out of work.

Fortunately, the black swan was not in danger of becoming extinct—especially in the west, where the black swan had become a symbol of our unique country. The first Western Australian stamp, printed in 1854, featured a black swan rather than a picture of Queen Victoria. The swan eventually became a symbol of Western Australia and is featured on the Western Australian coat of arms.

'a symbol of Western Australia'

In the eighteenth and nineteenth centuries, the black swan became a symbol of all that was strange and different in the Great South Land.

In 1697, a draughtsman named Victor Victorszoon drew this picture of Dutch sailors setting out in their longboats to catch black swans. The river shown is the Swan River which now flows through the heart of the city of Perth in Western Australia.

WHAT THE EUROPEANS NEEDED TO LEARN

The black swan is the only native swan in Australia, and the only truly black swan in the world.

Just the tips of their wing feathers are white, which can be seen when the bird is in flight. They are one of the largest flying birds in Australia, with a wingspan of up to two metres. The call of a black swan can sound very musical, almost like a bugle or trumpet, but they also make soft crooning and whistling noises, especially when caring for their young.

'THE CALL OF A BLACK SWAN CAN SOUND VERY MUSICAL'

Black swans are vegetarian, using their long necks to help them pick leaves and shoots growing in the marshes, swamps and rivers that are their homes.

They begin to breed from about 18 months of age, and each pair of swans usually bonds for life. They build their messy nests—a pile of reeds and grasses—in a sheltered spot, often on a small island or in the reeds of a waterway. The cygnets (chicks) have grey downy feathers and stay close to their parents for about six months, sometimes riding on their parents' backs for trips into deeper water.

Black swans are widely distributed in freshwater and briny swamps, rivers, estuaries, and lakes, but may also migrate to other areas in wet seasons. They are sometimes seen out at sea. Since European settlement of Australia, the black swan has been introduced to New Zealand and elsewhere. The bird that was once feared for its connection with black magic is now admired by bird lovers all around the world.

BLACK SWAN

BLACK SWAN
FAST FACTS

Common name:
black swan

Scientific name:
Cygnus atratus

Some historical names:
Dampier black-swan, Shawian

Some Indigenous names:
baiamul, koolyn, connewarre, berrima, mulgoa, muru-kutchi (Maroochydore on Queensland's Sunshine Coast is named for Murukutchi-dha, the place of the black swan)

Weight and size:
up to 146 cm in length; weighs around 6 kg; female slightly smaller

Size relative to a 2-metre-tall man:

Habits:
territorial when breeding; outside the breeding season, they travel large distances, very occasionally reaching New Guinea; flocks fly at night and rest during the day

Habitat:
throughout Australia, with the exception of the Cape York Peninsula and dry deserts; prefers large salt, brackish or fresh waterways and permanent wetlands, requiring 40 m or more of clear water to take off

BLACK SWAN

Diet:
vegetarian—mostly leaves and shoots of aquatic plants, occasionally pasture

Reproduction:
One brood of about five cygnets (chicks) a year. Sometimes two females lay eggs in the same nest, which makes a brood of 10 or so. Both parents share the care of the eggs and young cygnets.

Life span in the wild:
up to 40 years

Laughing Kookaburra

was known as {GREAT BROWN KINGS FISHER}

CAPE TOWN, SOUTH AFRICA, 1771

Joseph Banks was glad to be on dry land again. The voyage from New Holland had been terrible and many of the men on board the *Endeavour* had died of disease.

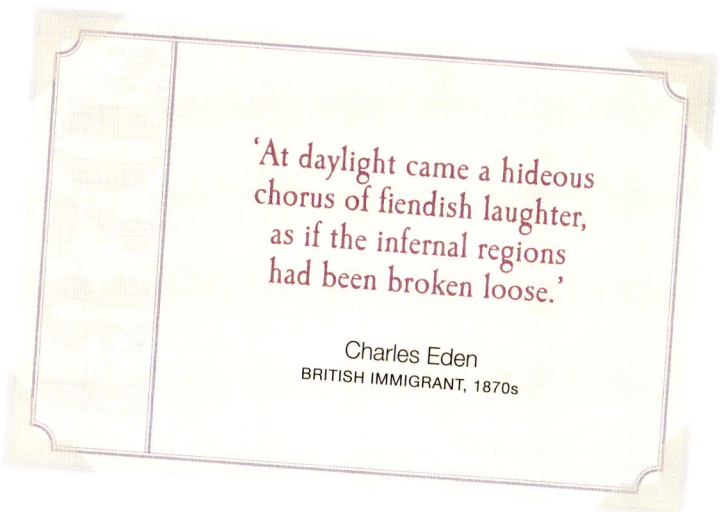

'At daylight came a hideous chorus of fiendish laughter, as if the infernal regions had been broken loose.'

Charles Eden
BRITISH IMMIGRANT, 1870s

The ship now lay anchored in the harbour at Cape Town, which meant that at last they were nearly halfway home.

While in Cape Town, Banks met a charming French naturalist, Pierre Sonnerat. Like Banks, Sonnerat was breaking a long voyage. When Sonnerat heard that Banks had collected many specimens from unexplored lands, he was keen to talk to him.

'I too am a scientist,' announced Sonnerat. 'I am on my way to New Guinea, Monsieur Banks.'

Banks was always happy to share what he had learned. 'You might like to see some of the specimens that I collected in New Holland,' said Banks. 'You'll find them of interest.'

The two naturalists discussed the strange and beautiful birds, animals and plants that Banks had observed. Banks even showed Sonnerat some of his specimens, including one of a large kingfisher.

'it laughs like a jackass'

'Extraordinary thing about this kingfisher is that it laughs like a jackass,' said Banks.

'It is a most impressive specimen,' said Sonnerat, admiring its speckled tail feathers. Even in its dried out state, it was a handsome bird.

'Then you shall keep it,' said Banks, offering the specimen to Sonnerat as a gift.

Sonnerat smiled and thanked Banks, but in 1776, when Sonnerat wrote about the 'Great King-Fisher', he didn't acknowledge Banks at all. He called the bird that Banks had given him the 'Grand Martin-Pêcheur de la Nouvelle Guinée' (Great King-Fisher of New Guinea). Sonnerat claimed that he had seen the kingfisher in the jungles of New Guinea, but in fact he had ventured only as far as Indonesia, and had then returned to France. In 1776, he published a book in which he included an illustration of the laughing kookaburra, claiming it as his own discovery.

The laughing kookaburra was given two scientific names in the course of the next century—*Alcedo novaeguineae* (meaning New Guinea kingfisher), by Sonnerat, and later *Alcedo gigas* (meaning giant kingfisher).

There are three other types of kookaburra found in New Guinea, but the laughing kookaburra lives only in Australia. Despite the fact that it is 100 per cent Australian, the laughing kookaburra is still referred to as *Dacelo novaeguineae,* simply because Sonnerat named it first.

THE BUSHMAN'S CLOCK

The kookaburra's common name was adapted from the Indigenous word used by the Wiradjuri people of south-west New South Wales who called it 'gugubarra'.

Many of the early settlers called the kookaburra the 'laughing jackass'. It was also known as the 'Hawkesbury clock' or 'bushman's clock'. Its early morning and evening laughter marked the beginning and end of every day for the settlers who had no clocks to help them tell the time.

Despite its cheerful call, the kookaburra was not popular with all the settlers. Its habit of occasionally raiding the nests of other birds, including the chickens that the settlers kept for eggs, and stealing both chicks and eggs, meant it was a target for shooting. Other settlers found its laugh unnerving. When Captain Charles Sturt was camped on the banks of the Murrumbidgee in 1830, he wrote that the kookaburra's cry was startling, 'as if laughing and mocking at my misfortune'.

'the kookaburra was not popular with all the settlers'

Grand martin-Pêcheur de la nouvelle Guinée.

The tide began to turn in favour of the cheeky bird when the settlers noticed that the kookaburra ate snakes. Once its reputation as a useful snake killer took hold, the settlers held their gun fire, and even went so far as to introduce the kookaburra to Western Australia and Tasmania, where it is not native. Its introduction in Western Australia created problems for both farmers and local wildlife.

'The tide began to turn in favour of the cheeky bird'

Despite the ups and downs of its popularity, by the twentieth century, the bird that had once unnerved so many new arrivals had become a symbol of Australia. The laughing kookaburra was featured on coins, postage stamps, and used as a trademark for dozens of different products.

Centuries after Sonnerat made up his story about seeing a laughing kookaburra in New Guinea, the famous larrikin Australian bird is stuck with a misleading scientific name, *Dacelo novaeguineae*. If the kookaburra knew the muddled-up history of its name, it would probably have a good laugh.

WHAT THE EUROPEANS NEEDED TO LEARN

The kookaburra is one of the largest members of the kingfisher family. Its distinctive laugh is used to mark out its territory.

It has a large, strong beak that it uses to catch its prey. Kookaburras are carnivorous, which means they love to eat meat. Even though they are kingfishers, kookaburras rarely catch fish and prefer to eat lizards, small snakes, various insects and spiders, mice and newly hatched birds. They also love to steal meat from barbecues, whether it's a sausage on a hotplate or a chicken drumstick in the hands of an unsuspecting human.

'THEY ALSO LOVE TO STEAL MEAT FROM BARBECUES'

Kookaburras live and hunt in family groups across Australia, and although they may look cheerful they can also be really aggressive. They love to squabble and fight. In one-third of nests, the older, stronger chicks will even kill their younger brothers and sisters.

LAUGHING KOOKABURRA

LAUGHING KOOKABURRA FAST FACTS

Common name:
laughing kookaburra

Scientific name:
Dacelo novaeguineae

Some historical names:
great brown kings fisher, Hawkesbury clock, bushman's clock, laughing jackass, giant kingfisher

Some Indigenous names:
gugubarra, goo-ginne-gan, gugagaga, kho-khoo-kha-kha

Weight and size:
up to 47 cm in length; weighs up to 0.4 kg; males smaller

Size relative to a 2-metre-tall man:

Habits:
territorial, living and hunting in family groups

Habitat:
woodlands and farmland of eastern Australia; introduced to south-west Australia and Tasmania

LAUGHING KOOKABURRA

Diet:
carnivorous — eats lizards, worms, small snakes, insects, mice and young birds

Reproduction:
It is common for kookaburras to bond for life. They share the parenting of their chicks, often helped by other male members of the family. The female lays up to five white eggs (usually three) each season in the hole of a tree.

Life span in the wild:
up to 15 years

Superb Lyrebird

was known as {MOUNTAIN PHEASANT}

PORT JACKSON, 1798

Governor Hunter wasn't sure if he could trust the young convict that stood before him. John Wilson was a wild tear-away character who would never do what he was told.

At one stage, he had run away from the convict settlement and lived with Aboriginal people. Wilson told wild tales of seeing weird creatures in the bush, including a peculiar new type of pheasant. Some of the men in the colony thought Wilson had invented the story to gain favour with the governor. Everyone knew Governor John Hunter was interested in the animals of the new land.

Hunter's latest problem wasn't deciding whether Wilson was telling the truth or not. A group of Irish prisoners had been spreading other stories, crazy stories about a strange colony of free white settlers living in luxury several hundred miles south of Port Jackson. The story was causing so much unrest that Hunter decided to send a party to explore whether there was any truth in the tale. The wild young John Wilson was sent along as well.

Three weeks later, John Wilson and the party of explorers returned. They were tired, thin and exhausted. They hadn't found the fairytale settlement, but they had brought back something that was of much more interest to Governor Hunter. Though the story of the fabled settlement

was a lie, John Wilson had told the truth about the shy pheasant, and this time he'd come back with proof.

Governor Hunter examined the bird. As Wilson had claimed, it was about the size of a pheasant but its tail was more like a peacock's, with two large, long feathers coloured white, orange and a lead-grey colour, tipped with black at the end. The body was brown and green, and its head and legs were black.

When Governor Hunter sent a box back to England with a specimen of a wombat and platypus, he included a pair of lyrebirds and one of its eggs, along with a note that read: 'they appear to me to be a species of the Bird of Paradise'.

The lyrebird had been 'discovered'.

> 'I scarcely ever heard of such devoted attentions as I one day witnessed in this noble bird towards his mate. I saw her sitting in the heat of the meridian sun upon her nest, and the cock bird seated near her, with his tail expanded, like a bower overshadowing her.'
>
> Rev. Richard Cobbold
> FROM *THE HISTORY OF MARGARET CATCHPOLE*, 1846

'its tail was more like a peacock's, with two large, long feathers coloured white, orange and a lead-grey colour'

☞ **Lyrebirds are very shy and will run away quickly if they sense a threat.**

73

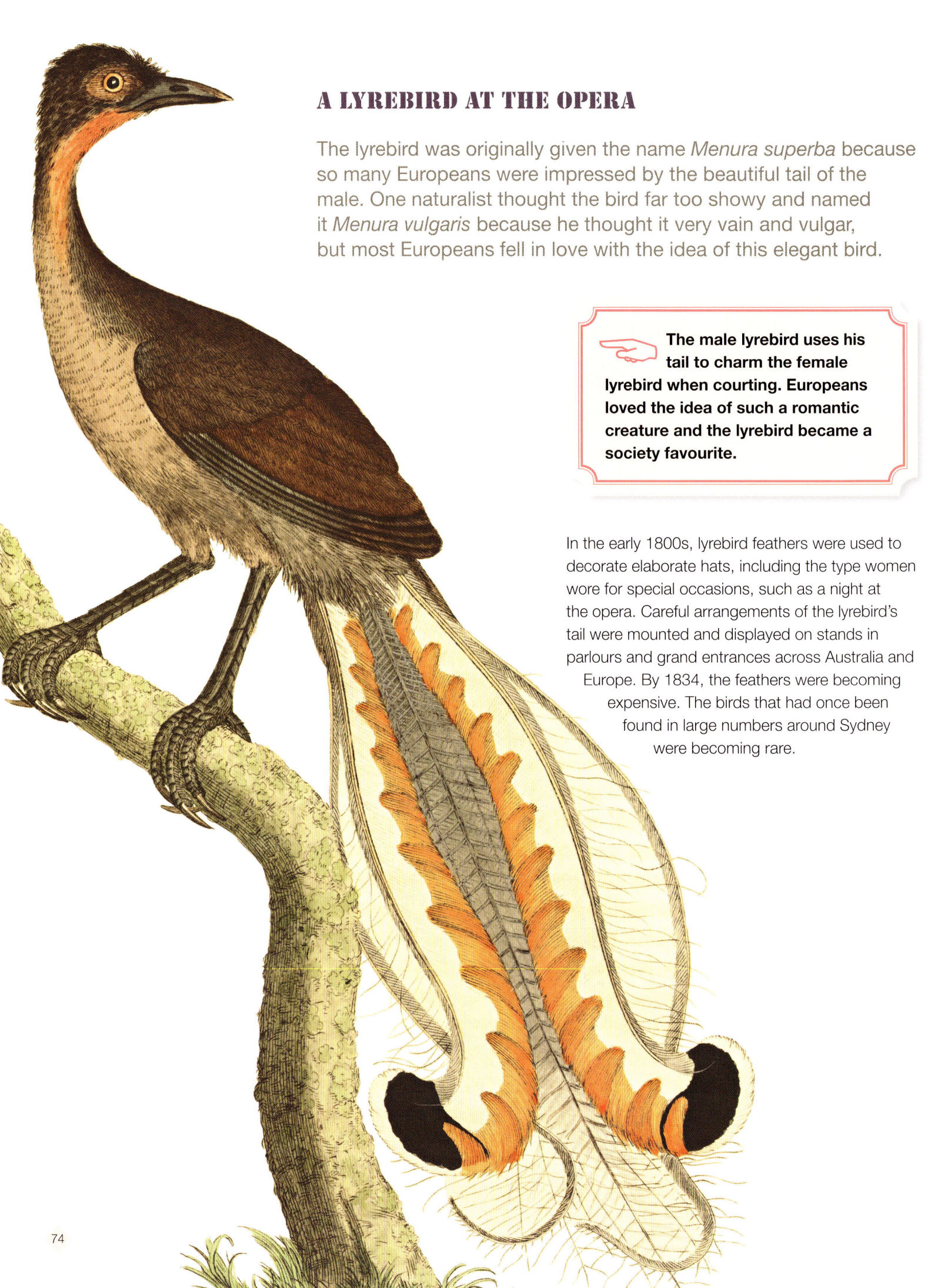

A LYREBIRD AT THE OPERA

The lyrebird was originally given the name *Menura superba* because so many Europeans were impressed by the beautiful tail of the male. One naturalist thought the bird far too showy and named it *Menura vulgaris* because he thought it very vain and vulgar, but most Europeans fell in love with the idea of this elegant bird.

☞ **The male lyrebird uses his tail to charm the female lyrebird when courting. Europeans loved the idea of such a romantic creature and the lyrebird became a society favourite.**

In the early 1800s, lyrebird feathers were used to decorate elaborate hats, including the type women wore for special occasions, such as a night at the opera. Careful arrangements of the lyrebird's tail were mounted and displayed on stands in parlours and grand entrances across Australia and Europe. By 1834, the feathers were becoming expensive. The birds that had once been found in large numbers around Sydney were becoming rare.

Perhaps if they'd had a chance to see the shy lyrebird in its native setting, the Europeans would have been even more impressed by its other charms, rather than simply by its feathers. Lyrebirds have an amazing ability to copy every sound they hear. They have their own song, but attract their mate by mimicking sounds in the forest. They can imitate the call of over 20 different species of birds. With the arrival of the Europeans, the lyrebird developed even more sounds. These days, lyrebirds are skilled at imitating many man-made machines, from lawnmowers through to chainsaws.

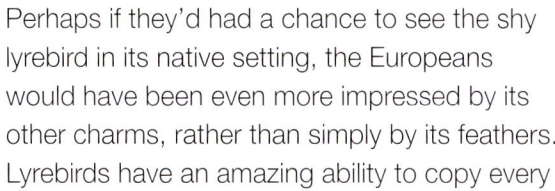

'Lyrebirds have an amazing ability to copy every sound they hear'

With its beautifully shaped tail, almost like a classical Greek lyre, the lyrebird was a perfect subject for artists. Drawings of the male lyrebird began to appear on books, artworks and ornaments from the early 1800s.

Early Europeans found the sounds of Australian forests disturbing. The cries of the birds seemed harsh and unmusical compared with what they were used to, and the dawn chorus that included the 'fiendish laughter' of the kookaburra upset many wandering Europeans. For settlers lost in dense bush, one of the most disturbing cries in the forest was often that of the lyrebird. Not only can the lyrebird imitate the sounds of other birds and machines, but it can also mimic perfectly the sound of a crying child or a screaming baby.

John and Elizabeth Gould created this beautiful image but they probably never saw a male lyrebird displaying his tail. In real life, the only time a lyrebird holds his tail upright is when he is courting, when he fans his tail out and over his head and back.

WHAT THE EUROPEANS NEEDED TO LEARN

It would be a long time after settlement before the Europeans discovered there are two lyrebirds in Australia.

The superb lyrebird, which is by far the most common, and Albert's lyrebird (*Menura alberta*). Albert's lyrebird was named for Queen Victoria's husband, Prince Albert.

Despite the fact that lyrebirds were so widely hunted, there was still a lot of confusion about the lyrebird's nest and eggs. In 1834, one zoologist said the nest was made of grass and leaves scraped together and that it contained 12 to 16 white speckled eggs. Twelve years later, another zoologist set the record straight. Lyrebirds lay only one egg that may vary in colour from a light grey to a deep purplish brown with dark grey streaks or spots.

When the male lyrebird is trying to charm his mate, he builds several mounds on which to perform. He courts the female lyrebird with his song and by spreading out his beautiful fan-shaped tail.

Lyrebirds' long tails make it difficult for them to fly and their wings are weak. They can fly a very short distance but mostly use their wings to help them jump through the forest as they run.

Luckily for the lyrebird, their shyness helped keep them alive long enough for laws to be passed making it illegal to hunt them.

SUPERB LYREBIRD
FAST FACTS

Common name:
superb lyrebird

Scientific name:
Menura novaehollandiae

Some historical names:
mountain pheasant, native pheasant, bird of paradise, superb menura

Some Indigenous names:
bulln-bulln, weringerong, woorail, beleck-beleck

Weight and size:
male up to 1.5 m in length, including the tail; female up to 86 cm (does not have fancy tail); weighs nearly 1 kg, on average

Size relative to a 2-metre-tall man:

Habits:
mostly walks, bounds or glides over the ground, only flies for very short distances; roosts at night in trees; very shy and will run away if threatened

Habitat:
lives in the undergrowth of the temperate woodlands, forests and rainforests of south-eastern Australia; introduced to southern Tasmania

SUPERB LYREBIRD

Diet:
scratches in the litter for insects, worms and other small creatures

Reproduction:
One egg is laid by the female in a bulky woven nest of twigs, fern, moss, leaves and bark. The nest is usually low to the ground amongst rocks or in a tree stump, but may be higher up where humans or foxes are a threat.

Life span in the wild:
about 15 years

Frilled Lizard

was known as { *CHLAMYDOSAURUS* }

WESTERN AUSTRALIA, 1820

Allan Cunningham was excited. Something very odd had caught his attention. Ahead of him, basking in the sunlight on the stem of a small, decayed tree was a lizard, but it was unlike anything Cunningham had ever seen before.

A flicker of movement caught his eye as the long, strange-looking lizard ruffled its collar. The lizard was fast, but Cunningham was faster. He caught the lizard before it had time to flare its huge collar out in alarm.

Cunningham was a member of the Phillip Parker King survey expedition that was charting the coastline of Australia in areas that Matthew Flinders hadn't managed to reach. He took the dead lizard back to camp and placed it amongst the other specimens he had collected.

'The lizard was the strangest thing he had found'

The lizard was the strangest thing he had found. It had a curious frill around its neck, covering all the way to its shoulders. When he pulled the collar out with his fingers, he discovered the neck frill was supported by long spines of cartilage, which were connected to the lizard's jawbone. Cunningham was sorry that he'd killed the lizard in his haste to catch it, as he would have liked to have seen it with its frilled neck flaring. Perhaps, though, if the lizard had flared its magnificent collar, he wouldn't have been able to catch it.

Cunningham's specimen of the collared lizard was the first recorded sighting by a European of the frilled lizard.

'I secured a lizard of extraordinary appearance ... it has a curious crenated membrane ... and when expanded ... spreads five inches in the form of an umbrella.'

Allan Cunningham
ENGLISH BOTANIST AND EXPLORER, 1820

Frilled lizards use their fancy collars to frighten their enemies, to win a mate and, possibly, to cool themselves.

THE DRAGONS OF OZ

George Grey was the first explorer to see the amazing frilled lizard in action.

Grey went on an expedition into the Kimberley ranges of Western Australia in the 1830s, but his attempts to capture the frilled lizard were made difficult by one very cranky reptile. The lizard looked so fiercely angry that all the men in the camp felt a little nervous. It threw itself up on its back legs and raised its head and chest as high as it could, so that no-one felt like trying to grab it. As it opened its mouth wide in warning, showing off a bright pink and yellow lining, its frilled collar flared out to reveal vivid orange and red scales. When the men still didn't retreat, the angry lizard made a fierce charge at Grey, as if it were about to bite. Grey took his chances and caught it—the first live frilled lizard to be caught by a European.

'its frilled collar flared out to reveal vivid orange and red scales'

Scientists were mystified by the frilled lizard. Was it a dragon that couldn't fly? Did it use its frills like a parachute to help it glide between trees? There were so many weird and unusual things about the new lizard that naturalists were at a loss to describe the reptile. The Europeans knew of no other lizard that ran on its back legs. It looked almost like a hen or a pheasant when it ran. Did that mean it was a bird-like reptile?

The frilled lizard is the largest Australian dragon. Depending on where it lives, it can vary in colour through shades of brown, yellow and red.

WHAT THE EUROPEANS NEEDED TO LEARN

In 1889, a live frill-necked lizard was taken to Paris for display.

Though lizards had once been considered creepy hairless monsters, reptiles were suddenly becoming fashionable additions to indoor fern gardens. Many people came to see the frilled lizard, but they were confused about the way it used its collar. One writer suggested it helped the lizard to fly when it jumped.

The large coloured and pleated skin flap, or frill, on the neck of the frilled lizard actually has several functions. While folded, the frilled collar acts as camouflage, making the lizard look like a ragged branch while it lies perched in a tree. The collar is also used in courtship and in competitions between rival males. As well, the collar may help to cool the lizard in the heat.

'THEIR COLLARS FLARE OUT AUTOMATICALLY WHEN THEY OPEN THEIR MOUTHS WIDE'

Frilled lizards try to make themselves look as scary as possible by opening their big mouths wide, hissing loudly, and charging their enemies at great speed. Their collars flare out automatically when they open their mouths wide. If the explorers thought this display was scary, imagine how terrifying it must be for the lizard's true enemies, such as eagles, owls, and dingoes.

It lives mainly in the dry tropical forests and grassy woodlands in northern Australia. It is often found in or near trees, mainly going onto the ground to hunt or to lay eggs. Like other lizards, it is most active during the warmth of the day.

FRILLED LIZARD

FRILLED LIZARD FAST FACTS

Common name:
frilled lizard

Scientific name:
Chlamydosaurus kingii

Some historical names:
frill-necked lizard, frilled dragon

Some Indigenous names:
booval (Kabi language), walumbi

Weight and size:
up to 0.9 m from head to tail; weighs around 0.5 kg; female slightly smaller than male

Size relative to a 2-metre-tall man:

Habits:
largely arboreal (tree-living); stays mainly in or near trees, but will go onto the ground to hunt or lay eggs; most active during the warmth of the day

Habitat:
lives in the dry forests and woodlands of northern Australia, from the Kimberley ranges of Western Australia to eastern Queensland; also found in southern New Guinea

FRILLED LIZARD

Diet:
termites, cicadas, beetles and other insects, as well as smaller lizards and other animals

Reproduction:
The female lays up to 25 tiny soft-shelled eggs in an underground nest. The eggs are incubated by the heat of the sun and the young emerge fully independent.

Life span in the wild:
about 20 years in captivity, but unknown in the wild

Pl. 65.

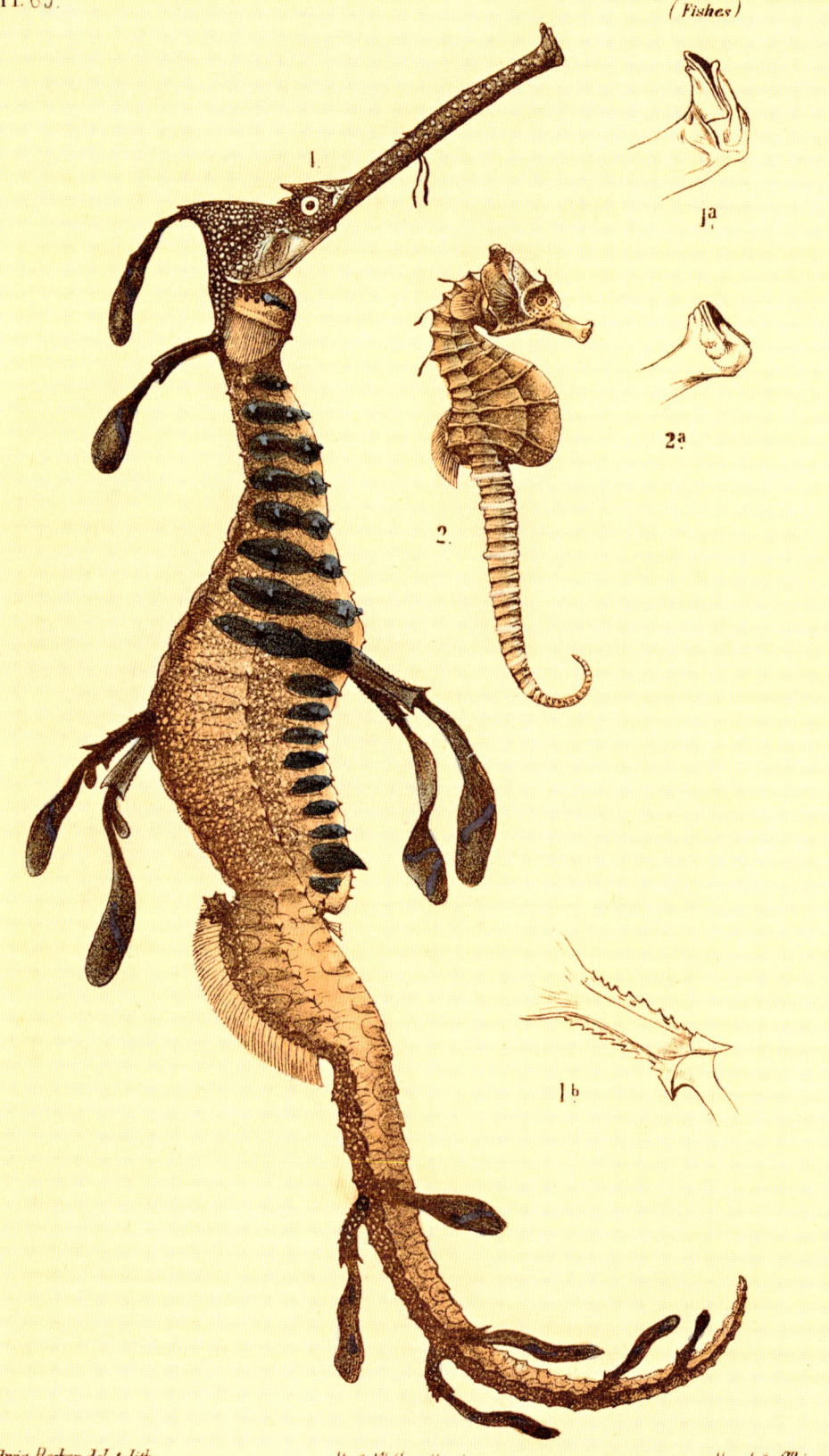

Sea Dragon

was known as {FOLIATED PIPEFISH}

KING GEORGE SOUND, 1802

Matthew Flinders was in no hurry to leave King George Sound. He had reached the south-west shores of Australia in December and had spent several weeks charting the coast, collecting natural history specimens and keeping an eye out for his French rival.

King Louis of France had ordered a French crew to map Australia's south, and the news had sent the British Government into a flurry of panic. Matthew Flinders was sent to finish charting the Australian coast for the British, to ensure the French didn't try and stake a claim on the Great South Land.

The clear blue sea sparkled in the January afternoon sunlight. Flinders lowered a dredge and trawl over the side of the ship and sailed back and forth across the harbour, netting small fish, shells, seaweeds and coral.

'It's a seahorse or some such fanciful thing'

Suddenly, one of the sailors cried out in surprise, 'Look here, Mr Bauer, you'll want to make a picture of this one. It's a seahorse or some such fanciful thing'.

Nestled in amongst the coral shells and seaweed was a beautiful golden sea creature. Ferdinand Bauer, the ship's artist, immediately reached for his sketchbook, while Robert Brown, the expedition's naturalist, began taking notes about the new discovery. The creature had a body formed of seven armoured segments, and the tassels that were attached to its tail, back and abdomen spread out around it like golden flames.

'A most extraordinary species ...'

George Shaw
BRITISH ZOOLOGIST, 1804

1804

Despite their amazing colours, sea dragons can easily be mistaken for a piece of seaweed.

Ferdinand Bauer's beautiful watercolour painting of the exotic new species captured the European imagination. The sea creature's wild colours and elegant shape were thought so fantastical, it could almost have been the inspiration for a real dragon.

OF SEAHORSES AND DRAGONS

In May 1804, a French naturalist descibed the new species as 'sygnathe de banderolles' or the streamered syngnathe.

Some scientists thought it a new type of seahorse but its mouth was like a long pipe and almost sealed shut at the end (syngnathe means fused jaws).

Because of its strange mouth, the British naturalist George Shaw decided it was a foliated pipefish, and that was the name that stuck for some time. It took many false starts and misunderstandings before scientists finally realised that the dainty sea dragon was neither a pipefish nor a seahorse, but a new type of fish.

'its mouth was like a long pipe and almost sealed shut at the end'

The long, leafy flaps on the sea dragons' bodies act as camouflage and protect them from their enemies.

WHAT THE EUROPEANS NEEDED TO LEARN

There are only two species of sea dragon—the weedy sea dragon *(Phyllopteryx taeniolatus)* and the leafy sea dragon *(Phycodurus eques).*

Although they are in the same family as seahorses and pipefishes, the Syngnathidae are in a class of their own. They are actually specialised marine fish.

Unlike seahorses, which swim upright, sea dragons swim like ordinary fish. They use their long skinny snouts to suck up plankton and sea animals, such as sea lice and tiny shrimps.

They are very timid yet graceful as they glide through the water with a swaying motion. Sea dragons can change their colouring according to their surroundings and their mood. They can change from a golden red with blue stripes to white spots and yellow markings. Unfortunately, they are not very strong swimmers and can often be found washed up on the beach after a storm. Early European beachcombers must have been fascinated by them because there is nothing quite like them in the Northern Hemisphere.

> **'SEA DRAGONS CAN CHANGE THEIR COLOURING ACCORDING TO THEIR SURROUNDINGS AND THEIR MOOD'**

Sea dragons usually breed in springtime. Unlike seahorses, male sea dragons don't have a pouch. Instead, they carry their eggs in a special brood patch on the underside of their tail. Before they mate, the male sea dragon prepares the area of his tail where he will keep the eggs. The female sea dragon pushes up to 250 eggs at a time onto the male sea dragon's tail, and he carries the eggs until they hatch two months later. The baby sea dragons are fully independent once they're hatched.

The number of sea dragons in the ocean is falling in some areas because of water pollution. It will be a very sad day if the sea dragons of Australia become as mythical as the dragons of fantasy.

SEA DRAGON

SEA DRAGON
FAST FACTS

Common names:
weedy sea dragon, leafy sea dragon

Scientific names:
Phyllopteryx taeniolatus,
Phycodurus eques

Some historical names:
foliated pipefish

Some Indigenous names:
none known

Weight and size:
weight unknown;
up to 45 cm in length (weedy);
35 cm in length (leafy)

**Size relative to a
2-metre-tall man:**

Habits:
very timid; will change colouring according to its surroundings; not a strong swimmer, tending to drift in the current like seaweed

Habitat:
lives in kelp forests, reef edges, seagrass meadows and seaweed beds of the shallow coastal waters of south-eastern Australia

SEA DRAGON

Diet:
tiny plankton, sea lice, larval fishes and shrimp-like crustaceans called mysids

Reproduction:
Male sea dragons carry up to 250 bright pink eggs at a time on the underside of their tails.

Life span in the wild:
up to 10 years

The Europeans

Some of the early Europeans mentioned in this book who observed Australia's wildlife

Joseph Banks (1743–1820) was a rich Englishman who sailed to Australia with Captain Cook. He kept a detailed diary of his time in Australia and was always interested in Australian animals and plants.

Ferdinand Bauer (1760–1826) sailed to Australia with Matthew Flinders. He made over 2000 sketches of Australia's plants and animals. Many of the specimens that Flinders collected were destroyed in a shipwreck, leaving Bauer's drawings as the only surviving record of what they saw during their voyage.

William Bligh (1754–1817) made many voyages to Australia and the South Pacific. In 1805, he was made governor of New South Wales, but lost his position during the Rum Rebellion. He is also famously remembered for a mutiny on his ship the *Bounty*.

James Cook (1728–1779) was a great sailing captain. He made three major voyages to the Southern Hemisphere. He wrote journals about his voyages and described many of the animals he had seen.

Matthew Flinders (1774–1814) was a great sailor who charted much of Australia's coastline. He wrote several books about his voyages.

George Grey (1812–1898) explored the north-west of Australia and wrote two books about what he observed. He became governor of South Australia.

George Prideaux Harris (1775–1810) came to Australia as a deputy surveyor in New South Wales. He moved to Tasmania in 1804 and wrote about the plants and animals he observed. He was the first European to describe the Tasmanian devil and the thylacine.

John Hunter (1737–1821) was a captain of one of the ships of the First Fleet. He later became the governor of New South Wales. Hunter drew pictures of the new animals he saw in the colony and sent them back to England, along with detailed descriptions.

Jacques Labilladière (1755–1834) was a French naturalist who travelled on a voyage to study and map Australia. The trip was ordered by King Louis of France so that France could consider making Australia a French colony.

Thomas Livingstone Mitchell (1792–1855) was an explorer and surveyor general of New South Wales. He made several important explorations of inland Australia and he published two books about his journeys.

Arthur Phillip (1738–1814) was commander of the First Fleet and the first governor of New South Wales.

George Shaw (1751–1813) was a famous English naturalist. He worked at the British Museum as assistant keeper of natural history. He wrote many articles about the strange specimens that were sent to him from Australia by the first settlers.

Pierre Sonnerat (1748–1814) was a French naturalist and explorer who made several voyages to South-East Asia. He never visited Australia but is responsible for the misleading scientific name of the kookaburra, *Dacelo novaeguineae.*

Willem de Vlamingh (1640–c.1698) was a commodore in the Dutch East India Company. He was sent to Australia to search for a missing ship. He arrived on the coast of Western Australia in 1696 and made notes about the animals he saw, including the black swan.

Information about every person named in this book can be found in history books or on the Internet. Hundreds of sailors, explorers, naturalists, Aboriginal people, and European settlers contributed to our modern understanding of Australia's wildlife.

GLOSSARY

The definitions below are as used in the book; check your dictionary for additional meanings.

arboreal
living in the trees

arid
very dry or parched from heat

bounty
a payment made for the killing of an animal

carnivorous
meat-eating

carrion
dead, sometimes rotted, animals or flesh

electro-receptor
an organ found especially in fish, but also in the platypus, that contains cells that can detect electric fields made by other animals. This helps the platypus to find prey

forage
to look for food or supplies

gender
whether something or someone is male or female

Great South Land
term used to describe Australia before it was fully mapped and named

habitat
an animal's natural environment

herbivorous
plant-eating

incubate
to sit on eggs in order to keep them at the temperature that the young inside need to develop and hatch

kelp
large, usually brown, seaweed

lair
where a wild animal shelters and rests

mammal
warm-blooded animals that breastfeed their young

marsupial
mammals that carry their young in a pouch

monotremes
mammals that lay eggs, that is, platypuses and echidnas

naturalist
somebody who studies nature

New Holland
Dutch explorers were the first Europeans to land on the western shores of Australia; they called the continent New Holland

nocturnal
active at night and sleeps during the day

nomadic
wanders from place to place

paradox
something puzzling and opposite to what it should be

predator
any meat-eating animal that lives by 'preying' on other animals

prey
animal hunted for food

quadruped
a four-legged animal

reptile
cold-blooded animals that lay eggs and are usually covered in scales; that is, snakes and lizards

scavenger
an animal that looks for dead animals or other edible scraps to eat

sonar
a method for detecting what is around you by sending out sound waves so they reflect off objects nearby

species
a particular type of plant or animal; within a species the individuals look similar to each other and can breed among themselves

squat
a shallow burrow, nest or resting place (also see lair)

succulent
a fleshy or juicy plant

taxidermist
someone who preserves and prepares dead animals so they can be stored and displayed; this may involve stuffing the skins of the animals and arranging their limbs

temperate
a climate that is moderate, with warm summers and cool winters

territorial
defending a territory, that is, stopping other individuals from entering the place where you live

vampire
a creature that feeds on blood

Van Diemen's Land
the first European name for Tasmania

Superb Lyrebird

Frilled Lizard

Sea Dragon

INDEX

NATIONAL
LIBRARY
OF AUSTRALIA

Published by the National Library of Australia
Canberra ACT 2600

© National Library of Australia 2012
Reprinted 2013
Text © Kirsty Murray

Books published by the National Library of Australia further the Library's objectives to interpret and highlight
the Library's collections and to support the creative work of the nation's writers and researchers.

National Library of Australia Cataloguing-in-Publication entry

Author:	Murray, Kirsty.
Title:	Topsy-turvy world : How Australian animals puzzled early explorers / Kirsty Murray.
ISBN:	9780642277497 (pbk.)
Notes:	Includes index.
Target Audience:	For primary school age.
Subjects:	Animals--Australia--Juvenile literature.
	Europeans--Australia--Attitudes--Juvenile literature.
Other Authors/Contributors:	National Library of Australia.
Dewey Number:	591.994

Commissioning Publisher: Susan Hall
Consultant: Penny Olsen
Editors: Susan Shortridge and Emma Gregory
Designer: Louise Dews
Image coordinator: Felicity Harmey
Research assistance: Fred Ford and Bill Geering
Production: Melissa Bush
Printed in China through Australian Book Connection

The National Library would like to thank the
Teacher Librarian Jane Stanton and the children
of Radford College Junior School for their help
in developing this book.

Acknowledgments

Topsy-turvy World is based on a beautiful book for adults
called *Upside Down World: Early European Impressions
of Australia's Curious Animals* (2010) by Penny Olsen.
The years of research and work that Penny invested in
Upside Down World made producing a version for younger
readers a straightforward and pleasurable task. I am very
grateful to her for providing me with such a fabulous book
from which to draw inspiration and material.

I'd also like to thank Susan Hall of the National Library
of Australia for realising the potential of a junior version
of *Upside Down World*. My understanding of Australia
as both my home and a land of unique beauty has been
enriched by working on such a great project.